The Quiet Spectrum: The Thought Patterns of Introverts

Shah Rukh

Published by Shah Rukh, 2024.

THE QUIET SPECTRUM: THE THOUGHT PATTERNS OF INTROVERTS

First edition. June 11, 2024.

Written by Shah Rukh.

Table of Contents

Prologue

In a world that often celebrates the loudest voices and the boldest actions, the quiet ones may seem to fade into the background. Yet, it is within this quietude that a unique spectrum of thought, creativity, and strength resides. This book, "The Quiet Spectrum: The Thought Patterns of Introverts," is a journey into the minds and hearts of those who navigate life with a contemplative approach, finding power in reflection and depth in solitude.

Introversion is not merely a personality trait; it is a rich and diverse experience, a spectrum of internal worlds that shape how individuals interact with the external one. For far too long, society has misunderstood and undervalued the introverted nature, equating quietness with shyness, and solitude with loneliness. However, introverts possess a remarkable ability to process information deeply, to think critically, and to create profoundly.

This book seeks to unravel the complexities of introversion, exploring the neurological, psychological, and emotional landscapes that define introverted thought patterns. It aims to provide a comprehensive understanding of what it means to be an introvert in a world that often seems to favor extroversion. By delving into scientific research, historical perspectives, and personal narratives, we will illuminate the strengths and challenges that come with a quieter disposition.

"The Quiet Spectrum" is not just for introverts, but for everyone. It is an invitation for extroverts to understand and appreciate the introverted minds around them, and for introverts to recognize and embrace their own unique gifts. Through each chapter, we will uncover strategies for thriving in various aspects of life, from personal relationships and social interactions to professional environments and creative endeavors.

As you embark on this journey through the quiet spectrum, I encourage you to pause, reflect, and listen—not just to the words on these pages, but to the silent whispers of your own inner world. In the following chapters, you will find a celebration of the quiet power that lies within, a power that is often overlooked but is undeniably profound.

Welcome to "The Quiet Spectrum." May you find inspiration, understanding, and a newfound appreciation for the beauty of introverted thought patterns.

Chapter 1: The Quiet Revolution

The concept of introversion has long intrigued psychologists, sociologists, and the general public. It is often perceived through the lens of a quiet revolution, an apt metaphor that captures the transformative and profound shift in understanding how introverts perceive the world and interact with it. This quiet revolution refers to a societal and personal recognition and appreciation of the introverted personality type, which has historically been misunderstood and undervalued in cultures that prioritize extroversion.

Introversion is a personality trait characterized by a preference for solitary activities, deep thought, and a limited but meaningful circle of social interactions. Unlike extroverts, who thrive on social engagements and external stimuli, introverts are more comfortable in environments where they can reflect, observe, and process information internally. This does not imply a lack of social skills or an aversion to socializing, but rather a preference for settings that are less overwhelming and more conducive to thoughtful engagement.

The foundation of understanding introversion lies in the work of Carl Jung, who first introduced the terms introversion and extroversion in the early 20th century. Jung's theory suggested that these traits are part of a spectrum, with individuals displaying varying degrees of each. He described introverts as individuals who are energized by their inner world of thoughts and ideas, rather than by external social interactions. This conceptual framework set the stage for subsequent research and exploration into the nature of introversion.

Over the decades, numerous studies have delved into the cognitive, emotional, and behavioral characteristics of introverts. One of the most notable findings is that introverts tend to have a different approach to information processing. They often exhibit higher levels of cortical arousal, meaning their brains are more stimulated by less intense external stimuli compared to extroverts. This heightened sensitivity can make introverts more prone to feeling overwhelmed in highly stimulating environments, prompting them to seek out quieter, less stimulating settings where they can recharge and engage more deeply with their thoughts.

Another key aspect of introversion is the quality of social interactions. Introverts typically prefer deep, meaningful conversations over small talk, and they value close, intimate relationships over a large social network. This does not mean they are antisocial or lack social skills; rather, they are selective about how they invest their social energy. This selective approach often leads to the development of strong, enduring relationships that are built on a foundation of mutual understanding and shared interests.

The quiet revolution in understanding introversion also challenges the traditional notions of success and leadership. For many years, societal norms have equated extroverted traits with effective leadership and success. Charisma, assertiveness, and a gregarious nature have been seen as essential qualities for leaders. However, recent research and real-world examples have demonstrated that introverted individuals can also be highly effective leaders. Introverted leaders often excel in roles that require thoughtful decision-making, active listening, and a focus on the needs and strengths of their team members. They are more likely to empower others, foster a collaborative environment, and lead with empathy and humility.

Moreover, the rise of remote work and digital communication has further highlighted the strengths of introverts. In settings where face-to-face interaction is less frequent, introverts can thrive by leveraging their strong written communication skills and ability to work independently. This shift has allowed introverts to contribute effectively in ways that align with their natural preferences and strengths, challenging the extroverted bias in traditional office environments.

The cultural narrative around introversion has also evolved significantly. The publication of books like Susan Cain's "Quiet: The Power of Introverts in a World That Can't Stop Talking" has played a pivotal role in raising awareness and appreciation for introverted traits. Cain's work emphasizes that introversion is not a flaw to be corrected but a valuable personality trait that offers unique strengths and perspectives. Her book and other similar works have sparked a broader societal conversation about the importance of embracing diversity in personality types and recognizing the value that introverts bring to various aspects of life.

In educational settings, the recognition of introverted traits has led to a more inclusive approach to learning and teaching. Educators are increasingly aware of the need to create environments that support different learning styles and preferences. For introverted students, this may mean providing opportunities for independent work, quiet reflection, and small group discussions, rather than relying solely on large, participatory classroom activities. This inclusive approach helps to ensure that all students, regardless of their personality type, can thrive and reach their full potential.

The quiet revolution also extends to the realm of mental health. Introverts, who often experience the world with a heightened level of sensitivity, may be more prone to anxiety and stress in highly stimulating or demanding social environments. Recognizing the unique challenges faced by introverts has led to more tailored approaches in mental health care, including strategies that emphasize the importance of creating safe, supportive spaces where introverts can process their emotions and experiences at their own pace. This understanding helps to reduce the stigma associated with introversion and promotes a more compassionate and individualized approach to mental health.

In the workplace, the quiet revolution is prompting organizations to rethink their approaches to team dynamics, communication, and professional development. Companies are beginning to value the contributions of introverts, recognizing that their ability to focus deeply, think critically, and work independently can lead to innovative solutions and high-quality outcomes. As a result, more organizations are implementing practices that support a diversity of work styles, such as flexible work arrangements, quiet workspaces, and opportunities for independent projects.

The quiet revolution in understanding introversion also underscores the importance of self-acceptance and self-awareness. For introverts, embracing their natural tendencies and preferences can lead to a greater sense of fulfillment and well-being. It involves recognizing that their need for solitude and reflection is not a sign of weakness, but a vital aspect of their personality that enables them to thrive in their own unique way. This self-acceptance is crucial for personal growth and for cultivating a life that aligns with one's values and strengths.

Ultimately, the quiet revolution is about shifting the cultural narrative to celebrate and embrace introversion as a valuable and important aspect of human diversity. It challenges the pervasive myth that extroversion is the ideal and acknowledges the rich contributions that introverts make to society. By fostering a deeper understanding of introversion, we can create a world that values and respects the full spectrum of human personality, allowing everyone to flourish in their own way. This revolution is not just about recognizing the strengths of introverts, but about creating a more inclusive and compassionate society that honors the diversity of experiences and perspectives that make us uniquely human.

Chapter 2: The Science Behind Introversion

The exploration of introversion has captivated scientists, psychologists, and researchers for decades, leading to a comprehensive understanding of the intricacies that define this personality trait. Introversion, in its essence, is characterized by a preference for inward focus and a propensity to be more reflective and reserved in social contexts. Unlike extroverts, who seek external stimulation and social interaction to feel energized, introverts often find solace and rejuvenation in solitary activities or small, intimate gatherings. This distinction is rooted in fundamental differences in brain function, neurotransmitter activity, and psychological processing, making the science behind introversion a fascinating subject that encompasses various aspects of biology, psychology, and social behavior.

At the heart of the science behind introversion lies the work of Carl Jung, a Swiss psychiatrist and psychoanalyst, who introduced the concepts of introversion and extroversion in the early 20th century. Jung's theory posited that introversion and extroversion exist on a spectrum, with individuals exhibiting varying degrees of each trait. Introverts, according to Jung, are more attuned to their inner world of thoughts and feelings, while extroverts are oriented towards the external world of actions and interactions. This foundational theory has paved the way for modern research into the biological and psychological underpinnings of introversion.

One of the key areas of investigation into introversion involves the study of brain activity and neuroanatomy. Research has shown that introverts and extroverts have distinct patterns of brain function that influence their behavior and preferences. A seminal study by psychologist Hans Eysenck in the 1960s proposed that the differences between introverts and extroverts could be attributed to varying levels of cortical arousal. Eysenck theorized that introverts have higher baseline levels of arousal in the brain's cortex, making them more sensitive to external stimuli. This heightened sensitivity means that introverts can quickly become overstimulated in environments with excessive noise, social interactions, or other forms of sensory input, leading them to seek out quieter, more controlled settings where they can manage their levels of arousal more effectively.

Further research using modern neuroimaging techniques has provided additional insights into the brain activity of introverts. Functional MRI (fMRI) and PET scans have revealed that introverts exhibit more activity in brain regions associated with introspection and planning, such as the prefrontal cortex. This suggests that introverts are more likely to engage in deep thinking, self-reflection, and careful consideration of their actions and decisions. In contrast, extroverts show greater activity in areas of the brain linked to reward processing and sensory perception, like the dopamine pathways. This difference in neural activation patterns helps explain why introverts tend to favor activities that are intellectually stimulating and require sustained attention, while extroverts are drawn to more dynamic and interactive experiences.

Another significant aspect of the science behind introversion involves the role of neurotransmitters, the chemical messengers that facilitate communication between nerve cells. Dopamine, a neurotransmitter associated with pleasure, reward, and motivation, plays a crucial role in this context. Research has indicated that introverts and extroverts have differing sensitivities to dopamine. Extroverts typically have a more active dopamine system, which drives them to seek out novel experiences and social interactions that provide a dopamine boost. Introverts, on the other hand, are less driven by dopamine and may even find that high levels of this neurotransmitter lead to overstimulation and discomfort. As a result, introverts often gravitate towards activities that are less likely to produce intense dopamine responses, such as reading, writing, or engaging in solitary hobbies that allow for quiet reflection and deep focus.

The neurotransmitter acetylcholine also plays a pivotal role in understanding introversion. Acetylcholine is linked to a state of relaxed alertness and the ability to focus attention for extended periods. Introverts tend to have a preference for activities that activate the acetylcholine system, which supports their need for calm, focused environments where they can engage in thoughtful analysis and introspection. This preference contrasts with the extrovert's inclination towards activities that stimulate the dopamine system, highlighting the fundamental differences in how these two personality types seek and process stimulation.

Genetics also contributes to the understanding of introversion, as studies have shown that personality traits like introversion and extroversion have a heritable component. Twin studies, which compare the similarities between identical and fraternal twins, have revealed that genetic factors account for a significant portion of the variance in introversion and extroversion traits. This genetic influence suggests that individuals may be predisposed to certain levels of introversion or extroversion based on their genetic makeup, although environmental factors and life experiences also play a critical role in shaping personality.

The role of the autonomic nervous system in introversion is another area of interest. The autonomic nervous system, which controls involuntary bodily functions, includes the sympathetic nervous system (associated with the fight-or-flight response) and the parasympathetic nervous system (associated with rest and digest functions). Research suggests that introverts may have a more reactive sympathetic nervous system, leading to heightened sensitivity to stress and external stimuli. This sensitivity can make introverts more prone to feeling overwhelmed in social situations or noisy environments, reinforcing their preference for quieter, more predictable settings where they can maintain a sense of calm and control.

Psychological research into introversion has also examined how introverts process information and make decisions. Introverts are often described as more deliberate and reflective in their decision-making processes. They tend to gather and analyze information thoroughly before arriving at a conclusion, which can lead to more thoughtful and considered decisions. This approach is reflected in their preference for environments that allow for deep thinking and uninterrupted focus, as opposed to the rapid-fire decision-making that is often associated with extroverted behavior.

The science of introversion also encompasses the concept of sensory processing sensitivity, a trait characterized by a heightened sensitivity to sensory input. Individuals with high sensory processing sensitivity, who are often introverts, may experience more intense reactions to sounds, lights, and other sensory stimuli. This heightened sensitivity can lead to a greater need for environments that minimize sensory overload and provide opportunities for quiet reflection and recovery. Understanding sensory processing sensitivity helps to explain why introverts may seek out low-stimulation environments and prefer activities that involve minimal sensory input.

In addition to these biological and psychological factors, the science behind introversion also explores the impact of cultural and social influences on introverted behavior. Cultural norms and values can significantly shape how introversion is perceived and expressed. In many Western cultures, which often emphasize extroverted qualities like sociability and assertiveness, introverts may feel pressured to conform to extroverted ideals, leading to feelings of inadequacy or social anxiety. In contrast, cultures that value introspection, mindfulness, and community harmony may provide a more supportive environment for introverts to express their natural tendencies and thrive.

The societal implications of introversion are profound, affecting various aspects of life, including education, work, and social relationships. In educational settings, understanding the needs of introverted students can lead to more inclusive teaching practices that accommodate different learning styles. For example, providing opportunities for independent study, quiet reflection, and small group work can help introverted students engage more fully and perform better academically. Recognizing the value of introverted traits, such as deep thinking and careful analysis, can also promote a more balanced and holistic approach to education that celebrates diverse ways of learning and knowing.

In the workplace, the science of introversion highlights the importance of creating environments that support different working styles and preferences. Introverts often excel in roles that require attention to detail, independent work, and the ability to think critically and creatively. By fostering a workplace culture that values quiet, focused work and provides opportunities for meaningful collaboration, organizations can tap into the strengths of introverted employees and enhance overall productivity and innovation. This approach also helps to counteract the bias towards extroverted behaviors, such as assertiveness and sociability, which can sometimes dominate traditional workplace dynamics.

Social relationships and communication are also influenced by introversion, as introverts often prefer deep, meaningful connections with a few close friends rather than a large network of acquaintances. Understanding the communication preferences of introverts, such as their need for thoughtful, one-on-one conversations and their aversion to small talk and social gatherings, can lead to more fulfilling and authentic relationships. By recognizing and respecting these preferences, friends, family members, and colleagues can build stronger, more supportive connections with introverts, fostering an environment of mutual understanding and respect.

The science behind introversion also extends to the realm of mental health, as introverts may face unique challenges related to their heightened sensitivity and need for quiet, reflective environments. Introverts may be more prone to experiencing social anxiety, depression, or stress in situations that demand high levels of social interaction or exposure to intense stimuli. Recognizing these challenges and providing appropriate support, such as therapy that focuses on building self-awareness and coping strategies, can help introverts navigate the demands of a predominantly extroverted world and maintain their mental well-being.

Chapter 3: Historical Perspectives on Introversion

Historical perspectives on introversion offer a fascinating lens through which we can examine how the understanding and societal perception of introverted behavior have evolved over time. From ancient philosophical reflections to modern psychological theories, the concept of introversion has been shaped by cultural, intellectual, and scientific currents across various eras. This exploration highlights the shifting attitudes towards introverted traits and the broader implications for how societies value different ways of thinking, interacting, and contributing to the collective good.

In ancient times, the roots of introversion can be traced back to early philosophical thought. Ancient Greek philosophers, particularly those influenced by the teachings of Socrates and Plato, placed a high value on introspection and self-knowledge. Socrates' famous dictum, "Know thyself," underscores the importance of inner reflection as a path to wisdom and virtue. Plato, in his dialogues, often contrasted the life of contemplation (bios theoretikos) with the life of active engagement in the world (bios praktikos), suggesting that the former, associated with introverted introspection, was a higher form of existence aimed at understanding eternal truths and the nature of reality.

In the Hellenistic period, philosophers like the Stoics and Epicureans further developed ideas that resonate with modern concepts of introversion. The Stoics, for instance, emphasized the importance of cultivating an inner tranquility and self-sufficiency that would allow individuals to remain undisturbed by external circumstances. This philosophical approach aligns with the introverted tendency to seek inner peace and resilience through solitary reflection and self-discipline. Similarly, the Epicureans advocated for a life of moderate pleasures and intellectual pursuits, suggesting that true happiness is found not in social status or material wealth but in the quiet enjoyment of simple, thoughtful activities.

During the Middle Ages, the perception of introversion was influenced by the dominant religious and philosophical doctrines of the time. Christian monastic traditions, in particular, celebrated the value of solitude and contemplation. Monks and nuns often withdrew from the worldly distractions of society to lead lives of prayer, study, and reflection. Figures like Saint Benedict and Saint Teresa of Ávila emphasized the importance of inner spiritual growth and the cultivation of a personal relationship with the divine, which required periods of solitude and introspection. This era, therefore, saw a reverence for the contemplative life, associating introverted behavior with spiritual depth and moral integrity.

The Renaissance brought about a renewed interest in humanism and the potential of the individual. This period celebrated the value of both solitary intellectual pursuit and active engagement with the world. Thinkers like Leonardo da Vinci and Michel de Montaigne exemplified the Renaissance ideal of the "universal man" who could excel in both reflective and social endeavors. Montaigne, in his Essays, delved deeply into his own thoughts and experiences, exploring themes of self-awareness and personal growth that resonate with the introverted inclination towards introspection. The Renaissance thus embraced a more balanced view of introversion and extroversion, recognizing the importance of both inner reflection and outward achievement.

The Enlightenment, with its emphasis on reason, individualism, and scientific inquiry, further shaped the understanding of introversion. Enlightenment thinkers such as René Descartes and Immanuel Kant valued the pursuit of knowledge and truth through rational thought and introspection. Descartes' famous assertion, "Cogito, ergo sum" ("I think, therefore I am"), reflects the primacy of inner consciousness and intellectual self-examination. Kant's philosophy, with its emphasis on autonomy and the moral law within, also highlights the importance of internal reflection and self-governance, key aspects of the introverted temperament. The Enlightenment thus fostered an intellectual climate that appreciated the role of introspection in the advancement of knowledge and ethical understanding.

The 19th century witnessed significant developments in the study of personality and individual differences, setting the stage for modern conceptions of introversion. The Romantic movement, which emerged in response to the Enlightenment's focus on reason and empiricism, celebrated the value of emotion, intuition, and the inner life. Romantic poets and writers such as William Wordsworth, Samuel Taylor Coleridge, and Ralph Waldo Emerson extolled the virtues of solitary reflection and communion with nature, emphasizing the importance of personal experience and inner depth. This period marked a shift towards a more subjective understanding of human experience, valuing the introspective qualities associated with introversion.

The 19th century also saw the emergence of early psychological theories that laid the groundwork for modern personality research. The work of Sigmund Freud, the founder of psychoanalysis, had a profound impact on the understanding of introversion. Freud's theories of the unconscious mind and the dynamics of inner psychological conflict highlighted the complexity of the human psyche and the importance of introspection in understanding oneself. Although Freud did not explicitly focus on introversion, his emphasis on the inner life and the exploration of unconscious motivations resonated with the introspective nature of introverted individuals.

Carl Jung, a student of Freud, made significant contributions to the understanding of introversion through his development of analytical psychology. Jung introduced the concepts of introversion and extroversion as fundamental personality orientations. According to

Jung, introverts are primarily oriented towards their inner world of thoughts and feelings, while extroverts are more focused on the external world of actions and interactions. Jung's work highlighted the value of both personality types and emphasized the importance of achieving a balance between inward and outward focus. His theories provided a framework for understanding the diverse ways in which individuals engage with the world and paved the way for further research into personality traits and differences.

The 20th century saw a proliferation of research into personality and the development of various models and theories that further elucidated the nature of introversion. The advent of psychometric testing and the development of personality inventories, such as the Myers-Briggs Type Indicator (MBTI) and the Eysenck Personality Questionnaire, allowed for more systematic study of introverted and extroverted traits. These tools provided a means to assess individual differences in personality and offered valuable insights into how introversion manifests in different aspects of behavior and cognition.

The work of psychologists such as Hans Eysenck and Raymond Cattell advanced the understanding of introversion by examining its relationship to other personality traits and its biological underpinnings. Eysenck's theory of personality proposed that introversion and extroversion are linked to differences in cortical arousal, with introverts having higher baseline levels of arousal that make them more sensitive to external stimulation. Cattell's factor-analytic approach identified introversion as one of the key dimensions of personality, further highlighting its significance in understanding human behavior.

The late 20th and early 21st centuries have seen a growing recognition of the value of introversion and a broader cultural shift towards appreciating diverse personality traits. The publication of books like Susan Cain's "Quiet: The Power of Introverts in a World That Can't Stop Talking" has brought widespread attention to the strengths and contributions of introverted individuals. Cain's work emphasizes that introversion is not a deficiency to be corrected but a valuable aspect of human diversity that offers unique perspectives and strengths. Her advocacy for the recognition and appreciation of introverted traits has resonated with many people and sparked a broader conversation about the importance of embracing different ways of thinking and interacting.

Modern research continues to explore the complexities of introversion, examining its implications for various aspects of life, including education, work, relationships, and mental health. Studies have highlighted the importance of creating environments that support the needs of introverts, such as providing opportunities for quiet reflection, independent work, and meaningful social interactions. This research underscores the value of understanding and respecting individual differences in personality and the need for inclusive practices that accommodate a range of preferences and strengths.

The historical perspectives on introversion reveal a rich and evolving understanding of this personality trait, shaped by cultural, philosophical, and scientific developments over time. From ancient philosophical reflections to modern psychological theories, the concept of introversion has been viewed through various lenses, each contributing to a deeper appreciation of the complexity and diversity of human behavior. By exploring these historical perspectives, we gain valuable insights into how attitudes towards introversion have changed and how we can continue to foster a more inclusive and supportive society that values the contributions of all individuals, regardless of their personality type.

Chapter 4: The Introverted Brain

The study of the introverted brain offers a compelling journey into the intricate workings of the human mind, revealing how introversion is not just a behavioral trait but a deeply rooted neurological phenomenon. Understanding the neurological basis of introversion provides valuable insights into why introverts think, feel, and behave the way they do. This exploration encompasses various aspects, including brain structure, neural activity, neurotransmitter dynamics, and sensory processing, all of which contribute to the unique cognitive and emotional landscape of introverted individuals.

At the core of the neurological understanding of introversion is the concept of cortical arousal, which refers to the level of activity in the brain's cortex. The cortex is the outermost layer of the brain responsible for higher-order functions such as thought, perception, and decision-making. Research suggests that introverts have higher baseline levels of cortical arousal compared to extroverts. This means that introverts' brains are more easily stimulated by their internal and external environments, leading to a preference for quieter, less stimulating surroundings where they can manage their levels of arousal more effectively. This foundational concept was first proposed by psychologist Hans Eysenck, who theorized that the differences in cortical arousal underlie the distinct behavioral tendencies of introverts and extroverts.

Further exploration into the brain's neural networks provides additional insights into how introversion manifests neurologically. One key area of interest is the prefrontal cortex, which plays a crucial role in complex cognitive processes such as planning, decision-making, and social behavior. Neuroimaging studies have shown that introverts tend to have more activity in the prefrontal cortex, particularly in regions associated with introspection and self-reflection. This heightened activity suggests that introverts are more inclined to engage in deep, thoughtful analysis and are better equipped to process complex information internally. The prefrontal cortex is also involved in the regulation of emotions and impulse control, which may explain why introverts are often perceived as more reserved and deliberate in their actions.

The default mode network (DMN) is another critical neural network implicated in introversion. The DMN is a network of brain regions that is active when the mind is at rest and not focused on the external environment, such as during daydreaming, self-referential thinking, and introspection. Studies have shown that introverts exhibit stronger connectivity within the DMN, indicating a greater propensity for internal thought processes and reflective thinking. This neural pattern aligns with the introverted tendency to seek solitude and engage in activities that allow for quiet contemplation and self-exploration.

The reward system of the brain, particularly the role of the neurotransmitter dopamine, is also central to understanding the neurological underpinnings of introversion. Dopamine is involved in the brain's reward and pleasure circuits, influencing motivation, reinforcement, and the pursuit of rewarding stimuli. Research has found that introverts and extroverts differ in their sensitivity to dopamine. Introverts typically have a less active dopamine system, making them less driven by external rewards and more sensitive to overstimulation. This lower sensitivity to dopamine may explain why introverts prefer activities that involve less social interaction and external excitement, favoring pursuits that provide intrinsic rewards, such as reading, writing, or engaging in solitary hobbies.

In contrast, extroverts have a more active dopamine system, which drives them to seek out social interactions and novel experiences that provide a dopamine boost. This difference in dopamine sensitivity highlights a fundamental distinction in how introverts and extroverts process and respond to stimuli. While extroverts are energized by external rewards and social engagement, introverts derive satisfaction from internal experiences and may find high levels of stimulation overwhelming.

The neurotransmitter acetylcholine also plays a significant role in the neurobiology of introversion. Acetylcholine is involved in promoting a state of calm, focused attention, and is associated with activities that require sustained concentration and thought. Introverts tend to have a preference for activities that activate the acetylcholine system, such as reading, meditation, and other forms of quiet, focused engagement. This preference aligns with the introverted need for environments that support deep thinking and uninterrupted focus, contrasting with the extroverted inclination towards activities that stimulate the dopamine system.

The autonomic nervous system, which controls involuntary bodily functions, also contributes to the neurological profile of introversion. The autonomic nervous system includes the sympathetic nervous system, responsible for the fight-or-flight response, and the parasympathetic nervous system, associated with rest and digestion. Introverts are thought to have a more reactive sympathetic nervous system, leading to heightened sensitivity to stress and external stimuli. This heightened reactivity can make introverts more prone to feeling overwhelmed in social situations or noisy environments, reinforcing their preference for quieter, more controlled settings where they can maintain a sense of calm and balance.

Another area of interest is the sensory processing sensitivity, a trait characterized by a heightened sensitivity to sensory input and environmental stimuli. Research suggests that introverts often exhibit higher levels of sensory processing sensitivity, meaning they are more attuned to subtle changes in their surroundings and more easily affected by sensory overload. This sensitivity can lead to a preference for low-stimulation environments and activities that minimize sensory input, allowing introverts to focus more effectively on their thoughts and feelings.

Genetic studies also provide valuable insights into the neurological basis of introversion. Twin studies have shown that personality traits, including introversion and extroversion, have a significant genetic component. Research has identified specific genes associated with neurotransmitter function and neural connectivity that may contribute to the development of introverted traits. For example, variations in genes related to dopamine and serotonin transporters have been linked to differences in sensitivity to reward and emotional regulation, which are key aspects of introversion. These genetic influences suggest that introversion is not solely a product of environmental factors but is also shaped by inherited biological characteristics.

The impact of early life experiences on brain development further underscores the complexity of the neurological basis of introversion. Childhood experiences, including the quality of parental care, social interactions, and exposure to stress, can influence the development of neural pathways and contribute to the emergence of introverted or extroverted traits. For instance, children who grow up in supportive, nurturing environments may develop stronger neural connections associated with emotional regulation and social engagement, while those exposed to chronic stress or adversity may develop heightened sensitivity to external stimuli and a preference for solitary activities. These early experiences interact with genetic predispositions to shape the unique neurological profile of each individual, contributing to the diversity of personality traits observed in the population.

The neurological insights into introversion also have significant implications for understanding mental health. Introverts, who may be more sensitive to stress and prone to rumination, are at a higher risk for certain mental health conditions, such as anxiety and depression. Recognizing the neurological basis of these vulnerabilities can inform more tailored approaches to mental health care, including strategies that emphasize the importance of creating supportive environments that reduce sensory overload and provide opportunities for quiet reflection and emotional processing. Understanding the neurological underpinnings of introversion can also help to reduce the stigma associated with introverted behavior and promote a more compassionate and inclusive approach to mental health.

The neurological insights into introversion have also influenced educational practices, highlighting the need to create learning environments that accommodate different cognitive and emotional needs. Introverted students, who may be more sensitive to sensory input and social dynamics, often benefit from classroom settings that provide opportunities for independent work, quiet reflection, and small group interactions. Educators who understand the neurological basis of introversion can create more inclusive learning environments that support the diverse needs of all students, fostering a culture of respect for individual differences and promoting academic success and personal growth.

In the workplace, the neurological understanding of introversion can inform practices that support the strengths and preferences of introverted employees. Recognizing that introverts may thrive in environments that allow for focused, independent work and minimize sensory distractions can lead to the implementation of flexible work arrangements, quiet workspaces, and opportunities for meaningful collaboration. By valuing the unique contributions of introverts, organizations can foster a more inclusive and productive workplace culture that leverages the diverse strengths of all employees.

The neurological insights into introversion also have broader societal implications, challenging the pervasive cultural bias towards extroverted traits and promoting a more balanced appreciation of different personality types. By understanding the neurological basis of introversion, we can recognize the value of introspection, deep thinking, and quiet reflection, and create a more inclusive society that honors and respects the diverse ways in which individuals engage with the world. This understanding can lead to more compassionate and supportive social practices, reducing the pressure on introverts to conform to extroverted norms and allowing them to contribute to society in ways that align with their natural preferences and strengths.

Chapter 5: Quiet Strengths

Introverts, often characterized by their preference for solitude and introspection, possess a unique set of strengths that are sometimes overlooked in a world that tends to favor extroverted traits such as assertiveness and sociability. However, the quiet strengths of introverts are profound and powerful, contributing significantly to personal success, professional achievement, and societal well-being. By examining these hidden powers in detail, we can gain a deeper appreciation of the value introverts bring to various aspects of life and the unique contributions they make to their communities and the world at large.

One of the most notable strengths of introverts is their capacity for deep thinking and reflection. Introverts often have a rich inner life, characterized by thoughtful analysis and introspection. This propensity for deep thought allows them to process information at a deeper level, leading to greater insights and understanding. Introverts are inclined to spend time contemplating complex problems, considering various perspectives, and developing well-thought-out solutions. This strength is particularly valuable in fields that require critical thinking and problem-solving, such as research, academia, and creative endeavors. The ability to think deeply and reflect on complex issues enables introverts to generate innovative ideas and make significant contributions to their areas of expertise.

In addition to their deep-thinking abilities, introverts often excel in areas that require focus and concentration. They have a natural ability to concentrate on tasks for extended periods without becoming easily distracted by external stimuli. This focus allows them to delve deeply into their work, achieving a level of mastery and expertise that can be difficult to attain for those who are more easily diverted by social interactions or external activities. Introverts' capacity for sustained attention makes them particularly effective in roles that require precision, meticulousness, and attention to detail, such as scientific research, writing, and technical work. Their ability to immerse themselves in their work leads to high levels of productivity and quality, often resulting in significant accomplishments and contributions to their fields.

Another hidden power of introverts is their ability to listen and empathize with others. Introverts tend to be good listeners, valuing the thoughts and feelings of those around them. They are often more interested in understanding others than in asserting their own opinions, which makes them approachable and trustworthy confidants. This strength is especially valuable in personal relationships, where the ability to listen and empathize can lead to deeper connections and more meaningful interactions. In professional settings, introverts' listening skills can enhance collaboration and teamwork, as they are able to understand and integrate diverse perspectives, fostering a more inclusive and productive work environment.

Introverts also possess a strong sense of self-awareness, which is cultivated through their tendency towards introspection. This self-awareness allows them to understand their strengths and weaknesses, set realistic goals, and make informed decisions about their personal and professional lives. Introverts are often more in tune with their emotions and can manage their responses to stressful situations more effectively. This emotional intelligence enables them to navigate complex social dynamics with sensitivity and tact, making them effective leaders and collaborators who can inspire and support their teams while maintaining a calm and composed demeanor.

The ability to work independently is another significant strength of introverts. They often prefer to work alone or in small, quiet environments where they can focus on their tasks without the distractions of a bustling social environment. This independence allows introverts to be self-sufficient and resourceful, capable of taking initiative and managing their work without constant supervision or external input. Their preference for solitary work can lead to high levels of creativity and innovation, as they have the freedom to explore new ideas and approaches without the constraints of groupthink or external pressures. This independence is particularly valuable in roles that require initiative and self-direction, such as entrepreneurship, research, and creative arts.

Introverts are also known for their ability to maintain a calm and composed demeanor, even in high-pressure situations. Their natural inclination towards reflection and internal processing enables them to approach challenges with a thoughtful and measured response, rather than reacting impulsively or emotionally. This composure allows introverts to remain focused and effective in the face of adversity, making them reliable and resilient leaders who can navigate complex and stressful situations with poise and confidence. Their ability to maintain a calm presence can have a positive impact on those around them, fostering a sense of stability and trust in team environments and leadership roles.

In addition to their calm and composed demeanor, introverts often possess a strong sense of empathy and compassion. Their introspective nature allows them to connect with others on a deep emotional level, understanding and appreciating the experiences and feelings of those around them. This empathy enables introverts to build strong, supportive relationships and to provide meaningful support and encouragement to their friends, family, and colleagues. In professional settings, this empathy can lead to more effective communication and collaboration, as introverts are able to understand and address the needs and concerns of their team members, creating a more inclusive and supportive work environment.

Introverts also have a remarkable ability to observe and analyze their surroundings, picking up on subtle cues and details that others may overlook. This observational skill allows them to gain a deep understanding of social dynamics and to identify potential opportunities and challenges that may not be immediately apparent. Introverts' keen observational abilities enable them to make informed decisions and to develop strategies that take into account a wide range of factors, leading to more effective and successful outcomes. Their attention to detail and ability to analyze complex information make them valuable assets in fields that require strategic thinking and problem-solving, such as business, research, and creative industries.

The strength of introverts in building deep and meaningful relationships is another important aspect of their hidden powers. Introverts tend to value quality over quantity in their social interactions, seeking out meaningful connections rather than superficial acquaintances. This focus on depth allows them to form strong, lasting relationships that are based on mutual respect, trust, and understanding. These deep connections provide a strong support network and contribute to a sense of personal fulfillment and well-being. In professional settings, introverts' ability to build and maintain strong relationships can lead to more effective collaboration and teamwork, as they are able to foster a sense of trust and camaraderie among their colleagues.

Introverts also have a natural ability to think creatively and to develop innovative solutions to complex problems. Their tendency towards introspection and deep thought allows them to approach challenges with a fresh perspective, considering a wide range of possibilities and exploring unconventional ideas. This creative thinking is particularly valuable in fields that require innovation and problem-solving, such as technology, science, and the arts. Introverts' ability to generate and develop new ideas can lead to significant breakthroughs and advancements, contributing to the growth and success of their organizations and communities.

The quiet strengths of introverts are further highlighted by their ability to adapt to changing circumstances and to remain flexible in the face of uncertainty. Introverts' introspective nature allows them to process and reflect on new information and experiences, enabling them to adjust their approach and strategies as needed. This adaptability is particularly valuable in today's fast-paced and ever-changing world, where the ability to navigate uncertainty and to respond to new challenges is essential for success. Introverts' ability to remain flexible and open-minded allows them to thrive in dynamic environments and to contribute to the success and resilience of their teams and organizations.

In addition to their adaptability, introverts often possess a strong sense of integrity and authenticity. Their introspective nature allows them to understand and stay true to their values and principles, leading to a consistent and genuine approach to their personal and professional lives. This authenticity fosters trust and respect among their peers and colleagues, as introverts are seen as reliable and honest individuals who are true to their word. In leadership roles, this integrity can inspire confidence and loyalty among team members, leading to a more cohesive and effective team dynamic.

The ability of introverts to communicate effectively through written and non-verbal means is another important aspect of their hidden strengths. While introverts may not always be as comfortable with verbal communication in social settings, they often excel in expressing their thoughts and ideas through writing and other non-verbal channels. This skill allows them to convey complex information clearly and effectively, making them valuable contributors in roles that require strong communication skills, such as writing, research, and strategic planning. Introverts' ability to communicate through written and non-verbal means also enables them to connect with a wider audience and to share their insights and ideas in a meaningful and impactful way.

Introverts' ability to remain focused and dedicated to their goals and passions is another key aspect of their hidden strengths. Their introspective nature allows them to identify and pursue their interests with determination and perseverance, often leading to significant accomplishments and success in their chosen fields. Introverts' dedication and commitment to their goals enable them to overcome challenges and setbacks, and to achieve a high level of expertise and mastery in their areas of interest. This focus and determination are particularly valuable in fields that require long-term commitment and sustained effort, such as academia, research, and the arts.

Chapter 6: The Introvert's Toolkit

The concept of an introvert's toolkit encompasses a comprehensive set of skills and strategies designed to help introverts not only navigate but thrive in various aspects of life. The unique strengths and preferences of introverts—such as their ability to focus deeply, think critically, and build meaningful relationships—are assets that can be leveraged to achieve personal and professional success. However, introverts often face challenges in environments that favor extroverted traits like assertiveness and sociability. The introvert's toolkit includes essential skills for self-awareness, effective communication, managing energy, and fostering personal growth, enabling introverts to harness their strengths and navigate the world with confidence.

At the foundation of the introvert's toolkit is self-awareness. Understanding one's own personality, preferences, and needs is crucial for navigating life's challenges and opportunities effectively. Introverts can benefit greatly from engaging in regular self-reflection, which allows them to gain insights into their thoughts, emotions, and behaviors. Techniques such as journaling, meditation, and mindfulness practices can help introverts develop a deeper understanding of themselves. This self-awareness empowers introverts to make choices that align with their values and strengths, leading to greater fulfillment and success.

Another essential skill for introverts is effective communication. While introverts may prefer listening over speaking and may feel drained by prolonged social interactions, developing strong communication skills can help them express themselves clearly and confidently. One aspect of this is mastering the art of active listening, which comes naturally to many introverts and can be a powerful tool in both personal and professional relationships. Active listening involves fully concentrating on the speaker, understanding their message, and responding thoughtfully. This skill not only enhances relationships but also fosters trust and respect.

In addition to listening, introverts can benefit from developing assertiveness. Assertiveness is the ability to express one's thoughts, feelings, and needs in a direct and respectful manner. For introverts, this can involve finding the balance between being overly passive and overly aggressive. Assertiveness training can help introverts communicate their boundaries and preferences without feeling guilty or anxious. This skill is particularly important in professional settings, where clear and confident communication can lead to better collaboration, job satisfaction, and career advancement.

Public speaking is another area where introverts can develop essential skills. While the idea of speaking in front of a group may be daunting, many introverts find that with practice and preparation, they can become effective and engaging speakers. Techniques such as thorough preparation, practice, and using visual aids can help introverts feel more confident and in control. Joining organizations like Toastmasters can provide a supportive environment for developing public speaking skills and gaining confidence.

Time management and organization are also critical components of the introvert's toolkit. Introverts often excel at tasks that require deep focus and concentration, but they may struggle with multitasking or managing multiple deadlines. Developing strong time management skills can help introverts prioritize their tasks, set realistic goals, and create a structured work environment. Tools such as to-do lists, calendars, and project management software can be invaluable in helping introverts stay organized and productive.

Energy management is another crucial skill for introverts. Because introverts tend to feel drained by social interactions and overstimulation, it's important for them to learn how to manage their energy effectively. This involves recognizing their energy levels throughout the day and planning activities accordingly. For example, introverts might schedule demanding or social tasks during times when they feel most energetic and reserve quieter, solitary activities for times when they need to recharge. Techniques such as taking regular breaks, practicing deep breathing exercises, and creating a calm, quiet workspace can also help introverts maintain their energy and focus.

Building and maintaining meaningful relationships is another area where introverts can thrive with the right skills. While introverts may prefer smaller, more intimate social circles, they can develop deep and lasting connections by being intentional about their relationships. This involves being selective about the people they spend time with, prioritizing quality over quantity, and nurturing relationships through regular, meaningful interactions. Introverts can also benefit from developing networking skills, which can help them connect with others in their professional and personal lives in a way that feels authentic and comfortable. This might involve one-on-one meetings, small group gatherings, or online networking, which can provide a more manageable and less overwhelming way to build connections.

Self-care and stress management are also essential components of the introvert's toolkit. Introverts often need time alone to recharge and process their experiences, and it's important for them to prioritize self-care activities that support their well-being. This might include practices such as meditation, yoga, spending time in nature, or engaging in creative hobbies. Stress management techniques such as deep breathing, progressive muscle relaxation, and mindfulness can also help introverts cope with the demands of daily life and maintain their emotional and mental health.

Another important skill for introverts is adaptability. While introverts may have a preference for certain environments and activities, the ability to adapt to different situations can enhance their resilience and success. This might involve stepping out of their comfort zone to take on new challenges, learning to navigate social situations with confidence, or developing strategies for managing change and uncertainty. By cultivating a growth mindset and being open to new experiences, introverts can expand their comfort zone and build greater flexibility in their lives.

Creativity is another area where introverts often excel, and developing creative skills can provide a powerful outlet for self-expression and problem-solving. Whether it's through writing, art, music, or other creative pursuits, introverts can tap into their inner resources to generate new ideas and solutions. Cultivating creativity can also provide a sense of fulfillment and joy, and it can be a valuable tool for personal and professional growth. Techniques such as brainstorming, mind mapping, and free writing can help introverts unlock their creative potential and develop new ways of thinking.

Leadership skills are also an important part of the introvert's toolkit. While introverts may not always seek out leadership roles, they often possess qualities that make them effective leaders, such as empathy, thoughtfulness, and the ability to listen and understand others. Developing leadership skills can help introverts lead with confidence and authenticity, whether it's in their professional lives, community involvement, or personal relationships. This might involve learning to delegate effectively, build and motivate teams, and communicate a clear vision and goals. By embracing their unique strengths and developing their leadership abilities, introverts can make a positive impact and inspire others.

In addition to these skills, it's important for introverts to develop a strong sense of self-advocacy. This involves recognizing their own needs and boundaries and being able to communicate them effectively to others. Self-advocacy can help introverts create environments and relationships that support their well-being and success. This might involve negotiating for flexible work arrangements, setting boundaries around social interactions, or advocating for their ideas and contributions in professional settings. By developing self-advocacy skills, introverts can take control of their lives and create conditions that allow them to thrive.

Finally, cultivating a sense of purpose and meaning is an essential component of the introvert's toolkit. Introverts often have a deep sense of introspection and a desire to understand the world and their place in it. Developing a clear sense of purpose can provide motivation and direction, helping introverts to align their actions with their values and goals. This might involve exploring their passions and interests, setting meaningful goals, and seeking out opportunities to make a positive impact in their personal and professional lives. By cultivating a sense of purpose, introverts can find fulfillment and satisfaction in their endeavors.

Chapter 7: Social Situations

Navigating social situations as an introvert can often feel like traversing a complex landscape filled with varying degrees of noise, both literal and metaphorical. The noise in this context refers to the overwhelming stimuli, constant chatter, and energetic demands that social settings typically impose. For introverts, who draw their energy from solitude and quieter environments, managing social interactions requires a set of nuanced strategies and an understanding of their own needs and limitations.

Understanding the nature of social noise is the first step. Social noise encompasses the loud and bustling environments often associated with gatherings, parties, networking events, and even everyday social interactions. For introverts, these settings can be particularly draining because their energy depletes with excessive external stimulation. The challenge is not just the volume of literal noise but also the mental and emotional demands of engaging with multiple people, processing conversations, and responding to social cues. Recognizing this helps introverts prepare themselves mentally and physically for such environments.

Preparation is key for introverts when it comes to navigating social situations. Unlike extroverts, who might thrive on spontaneous interactions, introverts benefit from planning and foresight. Before attending a social event, introverts can take time to understand the nature of the gathering, the people who will be present, and the expectations for interaction. This preparation can include setting personal goals for the event, such as aiming to meet a certain number of new people, reconnecting with specific individuals, or simply managing to stay for a set duration. By having a clear plan, introverts can reduce the anxiety associated with unpredictability and feel more in control.

One effective strategy for navigating social noise is to create a buffer zone of solitude before and after social engagements. Introverts need time to recharge their energy reserves, and carving out quiet time before heading into a social setting can help them feel more centered and prepared. Similarly, planning downtime after the event allows for decompression and reflection, helping introverts process their experiences and regain their energy. This might involve simple activities like reading, meditating, or taking a walk in nature.

During social events, finding moments of solitude within the gathering can also be beneficial. This can be as simple as stepping outside for a breath of fresh air, finding a quiet corner to regroup, or even taking a brief bathroom break to escape the noise and recharge. These small acts of self-care can provide the necessary respite to help introverts stay engaged without becoming overwhelmed.

Another important aspect of navigating social situations is understanding and leveraging personal strengths. Introverts often excel in one-on-one conversations and small group interactions. Rather than trying to engage with everyone at a large event, introverts can focus on building deeper connections with a few individuals. This approach not only aligns with their natural communication style but also results in more meaningful and satisfying interactions. By seeking out quieter spaces within the event and gravitating towards smaller groups, introverts can create an environment that feels more manageable and less overwhelming.

Active listening is a skill that many introverts naturally possess and can be a significant advantage in social situations. By focusing on truly hearing and understanding the other person, introverts can build rapport and trust. This attentive listening also allows introverts to guide conversations more comfortably, asking insightful questions and steering discussions towards topics they are passionate about. In this way, introverts can create dialogues that are both engaging and less draining.

It's also essential for introverts to develop and practice assertiveness in social settings. Assertiveness allows introverts to set boundaries, express their needs, and navigate interactions on their own terms. This can involve politely declining invitations to events that feel too overwhelming, excusing themselves from conversations when they need a break, or steering the conversation towards topics they find more engaging. By asserting their needs, introverts can protect their energy and avoid overextending themselves.

Managing the expectations of others is another crucial aspect of navigating social noise. Introverts can sometimes feel pressure to conform to extroverted norms, such as staying at a party until the very end or engaging in high-energy activities. Clear communication about their preferences and limits can help manage these expectations. For example, letting the host know that they might leave early or explaining to friends that they need quieter environments can reduce the pressure to conform and create more understanding and accommodating social dynamics.

In professional settings, such as networking events or conferences, introverts can employ specific strategies to navigate the social noise effectively. Networking is often perceived as an extroverted activity, but introverts can excel by approaching it strategically. This might involve researching attendees in advance, preparing thoughtful questions, and seeking out smaller, more intimate gatherings within the larger event. Following up with new connections via email or social media can also provide a less intense way to maintain relationships and continue the conversation on their own terms.

The use of technology can be a valuable tool for introverts in managing social situations. Social media platforms, professional networking sites, and messaging apps provide alternative ways to connect and engage with others without the immediate pressures of face-to-face interactions. Introverts can use these tools to initiate conversations, build relationships, and stay connected in a way that feels more comfortable and less draining. Virtual meetings and online communities also offer opportunities for introverts to participate in discussions and share their insights without the noise and intensity of in-person gatherings.

Self-compassion is an essential component of navigating social noise. Introverts may sometimes feel guilty or inadequate for not enjoying or thriving in social settings as extroverts do. Practicing self-compassion involves recognizing and accepting their natural preferences and limits without judgment. By being kind to themselves and acknowledging their unique strengths, introverts can build a positive self-image and reduce the internal pressure to conform to extroverted norms. This self-acceptance fosters a sense of confidence and authenticity in social interactions.

Developing a personal support system can also help introverts navigate social situations more effectively. Having a close friend or ally at social events can provide a sense of security and reduce anxiety. This support person can help facilitate introductions, provide companionship, and offer an escape route if needed. Additionally, being part of a supportive community, whether it's a social group, club, or professional organization, can provide a sense of belonging and reduce the feeling of being out of place in larger social settings.

Mindfulness and relaxation techniques can be powerful tools for managing the stress and anxiety associated with social noise. Practices such as deep breathing, progressive muscle relaxation, and mindfulness meditation can help introverts stay calm and centered in the midst of social stimuli. By regularly incorporating these techniques into their routine, introverts can build resilience and enhance their ability to navigate social situations with greater ease and confidence.

Ultimately, navigating social noise is about finding a balance that allows introverts to engage meaningfully with others while honoring their own needs and preferences. It involves a combination of self-awareness, preparation, boundary-setting, and self-care. By developing and utilizing their unique strengths, introverts can create a personalized approach to social interactions that feels both manageable and fulfilling. Celebrating and embracing their introverted nature is key to thriving in a world that often values extroverted qualities.

Chapter 8: The Art of Solitude

The art of solitude, often misunderstood and undervalued in a society that champions constant social interaction and extroverted traits, holds a profound place in the human experience. It is in these quiet moments, away from the cacophony of everyday life, that individuals can find true peace and a deeper connection with themselves. Solitude is not merely the absence of others, but rather a state of being where one can explore their inner world, reflect on their thoughts and emotions, and engage in activities that bring personal joy and fulfillment.

For introverts, solitude is not a retreat from life but a vital aspect of their well-being. Unlike extroverts who gain energy from social interactions, introverts recharge through alone time. This period of quietude allows them to process experiences, reflect on their lives, and indulge in creative pursuits without external pressures. The quiet moments provide a sanctuary where they can think deeply, cultivate self-awareness, and develop a rich inner life.

Solitude fosters creativity and innovation. History is replete with examples of artists, writers, and thinkers who produced their best work in solitude. Virginia Woolf, an iconic figure in literature, famously wrote about the necessity of a "room of one's own" for creative work. In these moments of isolation, the mind is free to wander, unbounded by social conventions or the immediate feedback of others. This freedom can lead to profound insights and original ideas that might not emerge in a more interactive setting.

In addition to creativity, solitude plays a crucial role in personal growth and self-discovery. Away from the influence of societal expectations and the opinions of others, individuals can explore their true selves. They can delve into their passions, values, and beliefs, gaining a clearer understanding of who they are and what they want out of life. This process of introspection can lead to greater self-confidence and a stronger sense of identity.

Moreover, solitude provides an opportunity for rest and rejuvenation. In the hustle and bustle of modern life, finding moments of peace and quiet can be challenging, yet they are essential for mental and emotional health. Solitude allows for a pause, a chance to breathe deeply and relax without the need to perform or engage. This downtime is crucial for reducing stress and preventing burnout. It offers a reprieve from the constant demands of work, social obligations, and the digital world.

The art of solitude also enhances one's appreciation of nature and the simple pleasures of life. When alone, individuals can immerse themselves in their surroundings, noticing details that often go overlooked in the rush of daily activities. A solitary walk in the park, the sound of birds chirping, the rustling of leaves, or the gentle flow of a stream can become deeply enriching experiences. These moments of connection with nature can foster a sense of peace and wonder, providing a counterbalance to the often-frenetic pace of modern living.

Furthermore, solitude can strengthen relationships with others. It might seem paradoxical, but time spent alone can improve the quality of interactions when one is with others. By understanding and fulfilling their own needs through solitude, individuals can engage more authentically and empathetically in social situations. They are better equipped to listen, support, and connect with others because they are not depleted by constant interaction. Instead, they approach relationships from a place of fullness and balance.

Practicing the art of solitude involves creating intentional spaces and times for quiet and reflection. This can be achieved through various activities such as reading, writing, meditating, or simply sitting quietly and observing one's thoughts. It might also involve setting boundaries with others to ensure that alone time is respected and preserved. In a world that often prioritizes busyness and connectivity, consciously choosing solitude can be a radical act of self-care and empowerment.

Solitude is not synonymous with loneliness. Loneliness is a sense of isolation and disconnection, while solitude is a chosen state that can lead to feelings of peace and contentment. Embracing solitude requires a shift in perspective, recognizing it as an opportunity rather than a deprivation. It is about finding comfort in one's own company and appreciating the richness that comes from within.

The benefits of solitude extend to all aspects of life, including professional endeavors. Many successful individuals attribute their achievements to the moments of solitude that allowed them to focus deeply and think strategically. Whether it is solving complex problems, planning future projects, or simply taking a mental break to avoid decision fatigue, solitude can be a powerful tool for productivity and clarity.

In essence, the art of solitude is about reclaiming a space for oneself in a world that is constantly vying for attention. It is about recognizing the value of quiet moments and the profound peace they can bring. For introverts, this practice is not only beneficial but essential for maintaining balance and well-being. However, everyone, regardless of their personality type, can benefit from incorporating periods of solitude into their lives. It is in these quiet moments that the noise of the outside world fades, allowing the whispers of the inner self to be heard. In the stillness, one can find clarity, inspiration, and a deeper sense of connection with the essence of who they are.

Chapter 9: Introverts in the Workplace

Introverts in the workplace often face unique challenges and opportunities due to their natural inclinations and preferences. Unlike extroverts who thrive on social interactions and external stimulation, introverts typically find energy and solace in solitude and quiet reflection. This fundamental difference in temperament can influence how introverts navigate professional environments, which are often designed with extroverted norms in mind. However, with the right strategies, introverts can not only succeed but also excel in their careers, leveraging their strengths to contribute meaningfully to their organizations.

One of the key strategies for introverts in the workplace is to understand and embrace their strengths. Introverts often possess qualities such as deep focus, strong listening skills, thoughtful communication, and the ability to work independently. These traits can be incredibly valuable in many professional settings. For instance, introverts' propensity for deep focus enables them to engage in complex problem-solving and detailed-oriented tasks that require sustained attention. Their strong listening skills make them excellent collaborators who can understand and integrate diverse perspectives, leading to well-rounded decision-making processes.

Thoughtful communication is another hallmark of introverts. They tend to think before they speak, which can result in more considered and impactful contributions during meetings and discussions. This quality is particularly beneficial in roles that require careful analysis and strategic thinking. Introverts' ability to work independently also allows them to excel in tasks that require minimal supervision and a high degree of self-motivation. By recognizing and leveraging these strengths, introverts can carve out a niche for themselves in the workplace where they can thrive.

Another important strategy is for introverts to create a work environment that suits their needs. This might involve arranging their workspace in a way that minimizes distractions and allows for periods of uninterrupted focus. For those who work in open-plan offices, this could mean using noise-canceling headphones, setting up a personal corner with privacy screens, or negotiating with management for the option to work remotely or in a quieter area. Having a workspace that supports their natural preferences can significantly enhance introverts' productivity and job satisfaction.

Managing energy levels is crucial for introverts in the workplace. Since social interactions and constant stimulation can be draining, it's important for introverts to schedule their workday in a way that balances solitary and social activities. For example, they might start the day with tasks that require deep concentration and minimal interaction, then schedule meetings and collaborative work for later in the day when they feel more prepared to engage with others. Taking regular breaks to recharge, whether through a short walk, meditation, or simply sitting quietly, can also help introverts maintain their energy levels throughout the day.

Effective communication is essential for success in any workplace, and introverts can benefit from honing their communication skills in ways that feel authentic to them. While they may not be the most vocal participants in large meetings, introverts can make their voices heard through written communication. Emails, reports, and memos provide opportunities for introverts to articulate their ideas clearly and thoughtfully. Additionally, introverts can prepare for meetings by planning what they want to say in advance, which can help them feel more confident and articulate during discussions. Finding a trusted mentor or colleague with whom they can practice and refine their communication skills can also be beneficial.

Building relationships and networking can be challenging for introverts, but it is a crucial aspect of professional success. Introverts might find traditional networking events overwhelming, but there are alternative approaches that can be more comfortable and effective. For instance, introverts can focus on building deeper, one-on-one connections rather than trying to engage with large groups. They can seek out opportunities for meaningful conversations during breaks or in smaller settings, where they feel more at ease. Leveraging online platforms and social media can also be a way for introverts to connect with others and expand their professional network without the immediate pressure of face-to-face interactions.

Introverts should also advocate for themselves and their needs in the workplace. This involves communicating their preferences and boundaries to colleagues and supervisors in a respectful and assertive manner. For example, if an introvert needs quiet time to complete a project, they should feel empowered to request that time and explain why it is important for their productivity. By advocating for themselves, introverts can create a work environment that supports their well-being and allows them to perform at their best.

Another strategy for introverts is to seek out roles and tasks that align with their natural strengths and interests. Jobs that involve research, writing, analysis, or creative work often provide the solitude and focus that introverts thrive on. Even within a role that requires some level of social interaction, introverts can look for aspects of the job that allow them to leverage their strengths. For instance, an introverted teacher might find fulfillment in preparing lesson plans and grading assignments, while an introverted manager might excel in one-on-one coaching and mentoring rather than large team meetings.

Developing a strong support system is also crucial for introverts. This can include forming relationships with colleagues who understand and respect their preferences, as well as seeking out mentors who can provide guidance and support. Having a network of trusted individuals can help introverts navigate workplace challenges and feel more confident in their professional environment.

Self-care is another important aspect of success for introverts in the workplace. Because introverts are more susceptible to burnout from excessive social interaction and overstimulation, it is essential for them to prioritize activities that help them recharge. This might include engaging in hobbies, spending time in nature, practicing mindfulness or meditation, or simply enjoying quiet time at home. By taking care of their mental and emotional health, introverts can maintain their energy and resilience, enabling them to perform effectively at work.

Lastly, introverts should continuously develop their skills and knowledge. Lifelong learning and professional development can enhance their expertise and confidence, making them more valuable assets to their organizations. Whether through formal education, attending workshops, reading industry-related materials, or seeking out new challenges within their current roles, introverts can stay engaged and motivated in their careers.

Chapter 10: Quiet Leadership

Quiet leadership, often seen as an oxymoron in a world that equates leadership with extroverted traits like charisma and assertiveness, offers a compelling and effective approach to guiding teams and organizations. This form of leadership leverages the inherent strengths of introverts, such as deep listening, thoughtful decision-making, and a preference for meaningful connections. Rather than relying on the traditional loud and dominant styles, quiet leadership emphasizes empathy, collaboration, and a steady, thoughtful presence. It is about leading with a calm, confident demeanor, and influencing others through example and inspiration rather than overt displays of power.

One of the most significant strengths of introverted leaders is their ability to listen deeply. Introverts are naturally inclined to listen more than they speak, which allows them to understand their team members' perspectives, concerns, and ideas thoroughly. This skill fosters a work environment where employees feel heard and valued, which can lead to increased engagement, loyalty, and productivity. Deep listening enables introverted leaders to gather diverse viewpoints and make well-informed decisions, considering all aspects of a situation before taking action. This thoughtful approach can lead to more innovative and effective solutions, as it incorporates the collective intelligence of the team.

Introverted leaders also excel in creating strong, one-on-one relationships with their team members. They often prefer meaningful, deep interactions over superficial ones, which can build a foundation of trust and respect. By investing time in understanding each individual's strengths, motivations, and aspirations, introverted leaders can tailor their approach to support and develop their team members effectively. This personalized attention helps in fostering a positive and nurturing work environment where employees feel empowered to contribute their best.

Another hallmark of quiet leadership is the ability to remain calm and composed under pressure. Introverted leaders tend to be more reflective and less reactive, which can be a stabilizing force during times of crisis or uncertainty. Their calm demeanor can help to soothe anxieties and provide a sense of stability for their teams. This measured approach allows introverted leaders to think clearly and strategically, making decisions that are in the best long-term interest of the organization rather than succumbing to the pressures of immediate, but potentially shortsighted, solutions.

Thoughtful communication is another key strength of introverted leaders. They often choose their words carefully, ensuring that their messages are clear, concise, and impactful. This can lead to more effective and meaningful communication within the organization. Introverted leaders are less likely to dominate conversations, instead encouraging others to share their ideas and opinions. This inclusive approach can foster a collaborative and innovative culture, where team members feel empowered to speak up and contribute.

Introverted leaders also bring a high degree of self-awareness to their roles. They are often introspective, regularly reflecting on their own performance and seeking ways to improve. This self-awareness can translate into a leadership style that is authentic and grounded, as introverted leaders are more likely to lead by example and practice what they preach. Their authenticity can inspire trust and loyalty among their teams, as employees can see that their leaders are genuine and committed to the organization's values and goals.

One of the challenges introverted leaders might face is the perception that they are not assertive or dynamic enough to lead effectively. However, quiet leadership does not mean a lack of presence or influence. Introverted leaders can develop their unique style that blends their natural strengths with the necessary elements of effective leadership. This might involve stepping out of their comfort zones at times, such as speaking up in meetings or advocating for their team's needs. Over time, introverted leaders can learn to balance their natural inclinations with the demands of their roles, finding a leadership style that is both authentic and effective.

Moreover, quiet leadership emphasizes the importance of empowering others. Introverted leaders often prefer to work behind the scenes, enabling their team members to shine. They focus on developing their teams, providing them with the resources and support they need to succeed. This approach not only enhances team performance but also fosters a sense of ownership and accountability among team members. By empowering others, introverted leaders can create a more engaged and motivated workforce.

Introverted leaders can also leverage their strengths in strategic thinking and planning. They are often skilled at seeing the big picture and thinking long-term, which can be invaluable for organizational success. Their reflective nature allows them to anticipate challenges and opportunities, and to develop thoughtful, strategic responses. This proactive approach can help organizations navigate complex environments and stay ahead of the competition.

In addition to these strengths, introverted leaders can benefit from certain strategies to enhance their effectiveness. One such strategy is to build a network of supportive relationships, both within and outside the organization. Having a trusted circle of advisors and mentors can provide introverted leaders with valuable insights and perspectives, as well as emotional support. These relationships can also help introverted leaders to expand their influence and impact, by connecting them with broader networks and opportunities.

Another strategy is to continuously develop their communication skills. While introverted leaders may not naturally enjoy public speaking or large group interactions, these are important aspects of leadership. By practicing and honing their skills, introverted leaders can become more comfortable and effective in these situations. This might involve seeking out training, working with a coach, or simply taking advantage of opportunities to practice in a supportive environment.

Introverted leaders can also benefit from creating structured opportunities for reflection and planning. Setting aside regular time for quiet reflection can help them to process information, develop insights, and make thoughtful decisions. This might involve maintaining a reflective journal, engaging in regular meditation or mindfulness practices, or simply setting aside quiet time each day for thinking and planning.

Balancing solitude and engagement are another key strategy for introverted leaders. While they need time alone to recharge and think deeply, they also need to be visible and engaged with their teams. Finding the right balance can involve setting boundaries around their time, such as scheduling regular periods for focused work, as well as making time for team interactions and relationship-building. By managing their energy effectively, introverted leaders can maintain their effectiveness and well-being.

Lastly, introverted leaders should embrace and celebrate their unique strengths. Rather than trying to emulate extroverted leadership styles, they should focus on what makes them effective and authentic as leaders. This might involve redefining success in their own terms, recognizing that their quiet, thoughtful approach can be just as powerful and impactful as more extroverted styles. By embracing their introverted strengths, they can lead with confidence and make a significant difference in their organizations.

Chapter 11: The Introverted Student

The introverted student, often characterized by a preference for solitary and introspective activities, approaches learning in ways that can significantly differ from their extroverted peers. Understanding the unique learning styles and strategies of introverted students is essential for creating an educational environment that supports their success and nurtures their strengths. Introverted students tend to thrive in environments that allow for deep thinking, reflection, and independent study, and they may struggle in settings that demand constant social interaction and immediate responses. By recognizing these differences and adapting teaching methods accordingly, educators can help introverted students achieve their full potential.

One of the primary characteristics of introverted students is their preference for solitary activities and environments where they can focus without distractions. They often excel in tasks that require concentration, such as reading, writing, and researching. Unlike extroverted students who gain energy from social interactions, introverted students may find that group activities and collaborative projects can be draining. To accommodate their needs, educators can provide opportunities for independent study and ensure that classroom environments include quiet spaces where students can work undisturbed.

Deep thinking and reflection are integral to the learning style of introverted students. They often prefer to process information internally before sharing their thoughts with others. This reflective approach allows them to develop a thorough understanding of the material and make connections between different concepts. Educators can support this learning style by incorporating activities that allow for reflection and thoughtful analysis. For example, giving students time to think about a question before requiring an answer, or encouraging them to keep reflective journals where they can jot down their thoughts and insights, can be highly beneficial.

Introverted students may also benefit from structured and predictable environments. They often prefer to know what to expect and may feel uncomfortable with sudden changes or spontaneous activities. Providing clear instructions, detailed syllabi, and consistent routines can help introverted students feel more comfortable and secure in their learning environment. This stability allows them to focus on their studies without the added stress of uncertainty.

In terms of classroom participation, introverted students might be less likely to speak up in large group discussions or volunteer answers spontaneously. This does not indicate a lack of understanding or engagement, but rather a preference for thinking before speaking. Educators can encourage participation by creating a supportive and inclusive atmosphere that values different types of contributions. Strategies such as small group discussions, written reflections, or online forums can provide alternative ways for introverted students to engage and share their ideas. These methods allow them to participate in ways that feel more comfortable and aligned with their natural inclinations.

Technology can be a valuable tool for supporting the learning styles of introverted students. Online learning platforms, discussion boards, and digital collaboration tools provide opportunities for students to engage with the material and their peers at their own pace. These tools can help introverted students feel more in control of their learning process and reduce the pressure of immediate social interaction. Additionally, using multimedia resources such as videos, podcasts, and interactive simulations can cater to different learning preferences and make the material more accessible and engaging.

Introverted students often excel in written communication, as it allows them to organize their thoughts and express themselves clearly without the immediate pressure of verbal communication. Encouraging writing assignments, research papers, and creative writing projects can play to their strengths and provide meaningful ways for them to demonstrate their knowledge and understanding. Furthermore, offering constructive feedback on written work can help introverted students improve their skills and gain confidence in their abilities.

Another important aspect of supporting introverted students is recognizing their need for downtime and mental breaks. Because social interactions and overstimulating environments can be draining, introverted students may require more opportunities to recharge. Allowing for short breaks during class, providing quiet areas for relaxation, and respecting their need for solitude can help introverted students maintain their energy levels and focus. Encouraging practices such as mindfulness and relaxation techniques can also be beneficial in helping them manage stress and anxiety.

Introverted students often have a strong preference for learning through observation and listening. They may benefit from lectures, demonstrations, and other forms of direct instruction where they can absorb information without the pressure to participate immediately. Visual aids, detailed notes, and step-by-step explanations can enhance their understanding and retention of the material. Educators can also provide opportunities for students to observe and reflect on their learning experiences, such as through case studies, simulations, or field trips.

In terms of assessment, introverted students may perform better with formats that allow for thoughtful and deliberate responses. Traditional timed exams can be stressful and may not accurately reflect their knowledge and abilities. Alternative assessment methods such as take-home exams, open-book tests, or project-based assignments can provide a more accurate measure of their understanding. These methods allow students to demonstrate their learning in ways that align with their strengths and reduce the pressure of timed performance.

Mentorship and one-on-one interactions can be particularly beneficial for introverted students. They often thrive in relationships where they feel understood and supported by a trusted adult or peer. Educators can foster these connections by offering office hours, personalized feedback, and opportunities for individual conferences. Mentorship programs, peer tutoring, and small study groups can also provide valuable support and encouragement. Building strong, supportive relationships can help introverted students feel more connected and engaged in their learning community.

Encouraging self-directed learning can empower introverted students to take ownership of their education. Providing choices in assignments, allowing for independent projects, and supporting their interests and passions can enhance their motivation and engagement. Self-directed learning fosters a sense of autonomy and responsibility, allowing students to pursue topics that interest them and to learn at their own pace. This approach can be particularly empowering for introverted students, who may prefer to work independently and explore subjects in depth.

Social skills development is another important area for supporting introverted students. While they may naturally prefer solitary activities, it is important for them to develop the skills needed for effective communication and collaboration. Educators can provide structured opportunities for social interaction that are respectful of their preferences. For example, pairing students for short-term projects, facilitating small group activities, and using role-playing exercises can help introverted students build confidence and improve their social skills. Providing guidance on effective communication strategies, such as active listening and assertive expression, can also be beneficial.

It is also important for educators to challenge the stereotype that introversion is a limitation. Introverted students bring unique strengths to the classroom, such as deep thinking, creativity, and attention to detail. By recognizing and valuing these strengths, educators can create an inclusive environment that celebrates diverse ways of learning and contributing. Encouraging a growth mindset, where all students are seen as capable of learning and growth, can help introverted students build confidence and resilience.

Parents and caregivers also play a crucial role in supporting introverted students. Understanding and respecting their child's temperament and learning preferences can help create a supportive home environment. Encouraging a balance between solitary and social activities, providing opportunities for quiet study time, and supporting their interests and passions can help introverted students thrive. Communication between parents and educators is also important to ensure that the student's needs are being met both at home and in the classroom.

Chapter 12: Parenting Introverts

Parenting introverted children requires a nuanced approach that respects their unique temperament and fosters their development in a way that aligns with their natural inclinations. Introverted children, who often prefer solitary activities and quiet environments, can sometimes be misunderstood in a society that values extroversion and social exuberance. Understanding the characteristics of introversion and adopting strategies that nurture their strengths while gently encouraging their social development can help introverted children thrive emotionally, socially, and academically.

Introverted children tend to be more reserved, reflective, and inward-focused. They often enjoy activities that allow for deep thinking and creativity, such as reading, writing, drawing, or engaging in imaginative play. These children may prefer spending time alone or with a small group of close friends rather than in large, noisy groups. They may also be more sensitive to external stimuli, finding loud environments or constant social interaction overwhelming. Recognizing these traits is the first step in effectively parenting introverted children.

One of the most important aspects of parenting introverted children is to create an environment that respects and supports their need for solitude and quiet time. This involves providing them with a space where they can retreat and recharge without interruption. A quiet room or a cozy corner with their favorite books, toys, or art supplies can serve as a sanctuary for them. It is essential to respect their need for downtime, especially after social activities or school, allowing them to decompress in their own way and at their own pace.

Listening and observing are crucial skills for parents of introverted children. These children may not always express their thoughts and feelings openly, preferring to keep them to themselves or process them internally. By being attentive and observant, parents can gain insight into their child's inner world and understand their needs and preferences. This means paying attention to non-verbal cues, such as body language and facial expressions, as well as providing opportunities for them to express themselves through creative outlets like drawing or writing.

Encouraging self-expression in introverted children can be facilitated by creating a safe and supportive environment where they feel comfortable sharing their thoughts and feelings. This involves being patient and giving them the time they need to articulate their ideas. Parents can encourage open communication by asking open-ended questions that invite more than yes or no answers and by validating their child's feelings and perspectives. It is important to create a non-judgmental space where the child feels heard and understood.

While respecting their need for solitude, it is also important to gently encourage introverted children to develop their social skills. Social interactions are a vital part of life, and helping introverted children navigate these experiences can build their confidence and resilience. This can be done gradually and at their own pace. Start by arranging playdates or social activities with one or two trusted friends rather than large groups. Participating in structured activities such as clubs, sports, or classes that align with their interests can provide a comfortable framework for social interaction.

Parents can also model social behavior by demonstrating effective communication and social skills in their interactions with others. Children learn a great deal by observing their parents, so showing how to engage in conversation, express emotions, and handle social situations can be very instructive. It is important to emphasize the value of listening and empathy, which are often strengths of introverted individuals, and to show that these qualities are just as important as speaking up and being outgoing.

Building self-esteem and confidence in introverted children involves recognizing and celebrating their unique strengths and achievements. Introverted children may excel in areas that require concentration, creativity, and attention to detail. Acknowledging their accomplishments in these areas and providing positive reinforcement can help them feel valued and capable. It is also important to avoid comparing them to more extroverted peers, as this can undermine their self-esteem and make them feel inadequate.

Encouraging independence is another key aspect of parenting introverted children. These children often thrive when given the opportunity to explore their interests and make choices on their own. Providing them with autonomy in certain areas of their life, such as selecting hobbies, managing their time, or organizing their space, can foster a sense of control and self-reliance. Supporting their interests and passions, even if they seem unconventional or solitary, can also help them develop a strong sense of identity and purpose.

Managing transitions and changes can be particularly challenging for introverted children, who may prefer routine and predictability. Parents can help by preparing their child in advance for any changes in their schedule or environment. Providing clear explanations and discussing what to expect can reduce anxiety and help the child feel more secure. Gradual transitions, where possible, are often more manageable for introverted children, allowing them to adapt at their own pace.

In educational settings, introverted children may require different approaches to support their learning and engagement. Communicating with teachers about the child's temperament and learning style can help ensure that their needs are met in the classroom. This might include allowing for quiet workspaces, providing opportunities for independent projects, and recognizing that these children may participate more in small group discussions than in large class settings. Encouraging teachers to offer positive feedback and support can also help introverted children feel more comfortable and confident in school.

Balancing structure and flexibility are important in parenting introverted children. While routines provide a sense of security, it is also important to allow for flexibility to accommodate the child's needs and preferences. This might mean allowing them to skip a social event if they are feeling overwhelmed or adjusting their schedule to include more downtime. Being attuned to the child's cues and needs can help parents find the right balance that promotes well-being and growth.

Parents of introverted children should also be mindful of their own expectations and attitudes. Society often places a premium on extroversion, and parents may feel pressure to encourage their child to be more outgoing. It is important to recognize and challenge these biases, understanding that introversion is a natural and valuable personality trait. Embracing the child's introversion and valuing their unique strengths can help them develop a positive self-image and a sense of acceptance.

Additionally, parents can seek out resources and support networks to better understand and support their introverted child. Books, articles, and online forums can provide valuable insights and strategies for parenting introverted children. Connecting with other parents of introverted children can also offer support and encouragement, as well as opportunities to share experiences and ideas.

Self-care for parents is also crucial when raising an introverted child. Parenting can be demanding, and ensuring that parents take time for their own rest and rejuvenation is essential. Practicing self-care allows parents to be more present and patient with their child, and it sets a positive example for the child to prioritize their own well-being.

Chapter 13: The Spectrum of Introversion

Introversion is a nuanced and multifaceted personality trait that exists on a spectrum, encompassing a wide range of behaviors, preferences, and dispositions. Understanding the spectrum of introversion involves delving into the various shades of quiet that define introverts and differentiating them from one another. While introversion is often oversimplified as mere shyness or social withdrawal, it is a much more complex and varied trait. It encompasses a broad array of characteristics and tendencies, all of which contribute to the rich tapestry of introverted personalities.

At its core, introversion is characterized by a preference for minimally stimulating environments and a tendency to turn inward for energy and focus. Introverts often find that social interactions, particularly in large groups or unfamiliar settings, can be draining rather than energizing. This preference for solitude and quiet does not imply a lack of social skills or a dislike for people; rather, it highlights a difference in how introverts recharge and where they derive their energy. Within this broad definition, there exists a spectrum that can be divided into different shades, each representing a unique manifestation of introversion.

One shade of introversion is the "social introvert." Social introverts do enjoy spending time with others but tend to prefer smaller, more intimate gatherings over large parties or events. They often have a close-knit circle of friends and feel most comfortable in familiar settings with people they know well. Social introverts may engage in social activities and enjoy meaningful conversations, but they also need time alone to recharge. They are not necessarily shy or anxious in social situations; instead, they simply find large groups and prolonged social interactions to be exhausting.

Another shade is the "thinking introvert." Thinking introverts are introspective and reflective. They spend a lot of time in their own minds, contemplating ideas, and analyzing their experiences. This type of introversion is less about social preference and more about cognitive style. Thinking introverts are often creative, imaginative, and thoughtful. They may enjoy solitary activities that allow them to explore their inner worlds, such as reading, writing, or engaging in artistic pursuits. Unlike social introverts, thinking introverts may not feel drained by social interactions, but they prioritize their inner lives and often need time alone to process their thoughts and ideas.

"Anxious introverts" represent another shade of introversion. Anxious introverts experience discomfort and anxiety in social situations, often due to self-consciousness or fear of negative judgment. This type of introversion is closely related to social anxiety disorder, but not all anxious introverts have a clinical diagnosis. They may avoid social interactions because they anticipate feeling awkward or inadequate. Even when alone, anxious introverts may ruminate on past social interactions and worry about future ones. Their preference for solitude is driven more by a desire to avoid discomfort than by a need to recharge.

The "restrained introvert" is another distinct type. Restrained introverts, also known as reserved introverts, tend to think before they speak and act. They are deliberate and measured in their responses and behaviors, often taking a while to warm up to new people or situations. This type of introversion is characterized by a slower, more methodical approach to life. Restrained introverts are not impulsive; they prefer to plan and reflect before making decisions. Their quiet demeanor may be mistaken for aloofness or indifference, but it is simply a manifestation of their thoughtful nature.

It is important to note that these shades of introversion are not mutually exclusive. Many introverts exhibit characteristics from multiple categories. For example, an individual might be a social introvert who also has a strong thinking introvert side. The spectrum of introversion is fluid, with individuals displaying different shades at different times or in different contexts. This variability highlights the complexity of introversion and the inadequacy of one-size-fits-all definitions.

Moreover, the spectrum of introversion is influenced by a range of factors, including personality traits, experiences, and environmental influences. Genetics play a significant role in determining where someone falls on the introversion-extraversion spectrum, but life experiences and personal choices also shape how introversion manifests in an individual. For instance, a person who grew up in a stimulating environment may develop different introverted tendencies compared to someone who grew up in a quieter setting. Cultural context is another important factor, as societal attitudes toward introversion and extraversion can influence how introverted individuals perceive themselves and how they are perceived by others.

The benefits of understanding the spectrum of introversion are manifold. Recognizing the different shades of introversion allows for a more personalized and empathetic approach to interpersonal relationships, both in personal and professional contexts. It helps to dispel common misconceptions about introverts, such as the notion that they are anti-social or lack confidence. By appreciating the diversity within introversion, we can foster more inclusive environments that respect and accommodate different personality types.

In the workplace, for example, understanding the spectrum of introversion can lead to more effective team dynamics. Managers can create environments that allow introverted employees to thrive by providing opportunities for quiet workspaces, flexible schedules, and independent projects. Recognizing that some introverts excel in roles that require deep thinking and creativity, while others may prefer tasks that involve detailed planning and reflection, can enhance productivity and job satisfaction.

In educational settings, teachers who understand the spectrum of introversion can better support their introverted students. Rather than forcing introverts to participate in large group activities or putting them on the spot, educators can offer alternative ways for introverted students to engage and demonstrate their understanding. This might include allowing students to work on projects independently or in small groups, giving them time to prepare before speaking in class, or providing written feedback instead of public praise.

On a personal level, individuals who recognize their own position on the spectrum of introversion can better understand their needs and preferences. This self-awareness can lead to healthier coping strategies and improved mental well-being. For instance, an introvert who understands their need for alone time can more effectively manage their energy levels and avoid burnout. They can also communicate their needs to others more clearly, leading to stronger and more supportive relationships.

Ultimately, the spectrum of introversion illustrates that there is no one-size-fits-all approach to understanding or accommodating introverts. The different shades of quiet each bring unique strengths and challenges, and acknowledging this diversity is key to fostering environments where introverts can thrive. By moving beyond simplistic stereotypes and embracing the full complexity of introversion, we can create a more inclusive and understanding world for all personality types.

Chapter 14: Introverts and Extroverts

Introverts and extroverts represent two ends of the personality spectrum, each with unique characteristics and preferences that influence their behavior, interactions, and experiences. The distinction between these two personality types has long been a subject of fascination and study, particularly in the fields of psychology and sociology. Bridging the gap between introverts and extroverts is crucial for fostering understanding, cooperation, and harmony in various social settings, including the workplace, educational environments, and personal relationships.

Introverts typically derive energy from solitude and quiet environments. They tend to be reflective, introspective, and focused on their inner thoughts and feelings. Social interactions, especially in large groups or noisy settings, can be draining for introverts, who often require time alone to recharge. This does not mean that introverts dislike people or socializing; rather, they prefer more intimate, meaningful interactions over superficial conversations. Introverts often excel in activities that require concentration, deep thinking, and attention to detail, such as writing, research, and creative pursuits. They may be perceived as reserved or even shy, but this is not always the case. Many introverts are confident and articulate when discussing topics, they are passionate about or when interacting in comfortable, familiar settings.

Extroverts, on the other hand, gain energy from social interactions and stimulating environments. They are typically outgoing, talkative, and assertive, thriving in group settings and dynamic, fast-paced situations. Extroverts often enjoy being the center of attention and are comfortable with expressing their thoughts and emotions openly. They are usually more spontaneous and may seek out new experiences and adventures. Extroverts excel in roles that require communication, teamwork, and leadership, as they are often skilled at motivating and inspiring others. They are perceived as sociable and approachable, which can make them effective in networking and relationship-building.

The fundamental differences between introverts and extroverts can lead to misunderstandings and miscommunications. Introverts may feel overwhelmed or overlooked in environments dominated by extroverts, while extroverts may perceive introverts as aloof or disengaged. These misunderstandings are often rooted in the differing ways introverts and extroverts process information and interact with the world around them. For example, an extrovert might interpret an introvert's need for solitude as a lack of interest in socializing, while an introvert might view an extrovert's enthusiasm for social gatherings as intrusive or overbearing.

Bridging the gap between introverts and extroverts requires a conscious effort to understand and appreciate these differences. One of the first steps is recognizing that neither personality type is superior to the other; both have valuable strengths and can contribute meaningfully to various contexts. Creating an inclusive environment that respects and accommodates both introverts and extroverts involves several key strategies.

In the workplace, fostering a balanced environment can lead to greater productivity, creativity, and employee satisfaction. For example, offering flexible work arrangements can accommodate introverts' need for quiet, focused time while allowing extroverts to thrive in collaborative settings. Providing spaces for both individual and group work, such as quiet rooms and open-plan areas, can help meet the diverse needs of employees. Encouraging a culture of respect for different working styles can also improve communication and reduce misunderstandings. Managers can benefit from training on personality differences to better support their teams and leverage the unique strengths of introverts and extroverts.

Educational environments can also benefit from bridging the gap between introverts and extroverts. Teachers can create inclusive classrooms by offering a variety of learning activities that cater to different personality types. For instance, incorporating both group projects and individual assignments allows students to engage in ways that suit their preferences. Providing opportunities for quiet reflection and discussion can help introverted students feel more comfortable participating. Additionally, teaching students about personality differences and encouraging respect for diverse traits can foster a more inclusive and supportive school culture.

In personal relationships, understanding and respecting personality differences is key to building strong, harmonious connections. Communication is crucial; partners, friends, and family members should openly discuss their needs and preferences. For example, an extroverted partner might need to understand an introverted partner's need for alone time, while an introverted friend might need to appreciate an extroverted friend's desire for social activities. Compromise and flexibility are essential, as both introverts and extroverts may need to adjust their expectations and behaviors to support each other. Celebrating each other's strengths and finding common ground can enhance mutual understanding and appreciation.

Another important aspect of bridging the gap is addressing and challenging societal biases and stereotypes. Introverts are often misunderstood or undervalued in cultures that prioritize extroverted traits, such as assertiveness and sociability. Recognizing the value of introverted qualities, such as deep thinking, creativity, and empathy, is essential for creating a more balanced and inclusive society. Similarly, extroverts should be appreciated for their enthusiasm, energy, and ability to connect with others. Encouraging a more nuanced understanding of personality can help reduce stigma and promote a more inclusive culture.

Technology and digital communication tools can also play a role in bridging the gap between introverts and extroverts. Online platforms and social media offer alternative ways for introverts to express themselves and engage with others on their terms. Virtual meetings and collaborative tools can provide introverts with more control over their interactions, allowing them to participate in ways that feel comfortable and manageable. At the same time, these tools can enhance extroverts' ability to connect and collaborate, making it easier to maintain social bonds and work together effectively.

In addition to these strategies, it is important to recognize that personality is not fixed. Many people exhibit a mix of introverted and extroverted traits, and individuals can develop skills and behaviors that help them navigate different social contexts. This concept, known as ambiversion, highlights the fluidity of personality and the potential for growth and adaptation. Encouraging people to explore and embrace both introverted and extroverted aspects of themselves can lead to more versatile and resilient individuals.

Ultimately, bridging the gap between introverts and extroverts is about fostering understanding, respect, and appreciation for diverse personality traits. By creating environments that accommodate different needs and preferences, promoting open communication, and challenging societal biases, we can build a more inclusive and harmonious world. Recognizing that both introverts and extroverts have valuable contributions to make can enhance our personal relationships, improve workplace dynamics, and enrich our communities. Embracing the full spectrum of human personality allows us to leverage the strengths of both introverts and extroverts, leading to a more balanced and dynamic society.

Chapter 15: The Quiet Revolutionaries

Throughout history, the world has been shaped by the contributions of many remarkable individuals, some of whom are recognized as quiet revolutionaries due to their introverted nature. These famous introverts have often operated behind the scenes, using their profound insights, creativity, and determination to drive significant changes in various fields. Despite the common misconception that introversion is a barrier to success, these individuals have demonstrated that introverts can achieve extraordinary feats and leave an indelible mark on the world.

Albert Einstein is perhaps one of the most iconic examples of an introverted revolutionary. Known for his groundbreaking contributions to physics, particularly the theory of relativity, Einstein's introspective nature and preference for solitary thinking played a crucial role in his scientific discoveries. He often retreated into deep thought, pondering complex problems in isolation. His ability to focus intensely and think deeply allowed him to develop insights that revolutionized our understanding of the universe. Despite his introverted nature, Einstein was able to communicate his ideas effectively, using his quiet confidence to influence the scientific community and beyond.

Another notable introvert who left a lasting legacy is Mahatma Gandhi. As a leader of the Indian independence movement, Gandhi's approach to activism was profoundly shaped by his introverted qualities. Unlike many political leaders who rely on charismatic oratory and public displays of power, Gandhi led through quiet determination and personal example. His philosophy of nonviolent resistance, or Satyagraha, required immense inner strength and self-discipline. Gandhi's ability to reflect deeply on issues of justice and morality, coupled with his preference for thoughtful, deliberate action, enabled him to mobilize millions and achieve significant social and political change without resorting to violence.

Emily Dickinson, one of America's greatest poets, was an introvert who found solace and inspiration in solitude. Dickinson's reclusive lifestyle allowed her to focus intensely on her writing, producing a body of work that explored profound themes of life, death, and nature with remarkable depth and sensitivity. Her introverted nature enabled her to observe the world from a unique perspective, distilling her experiences and emotions into poetry that continues to resonate with readers today. Despite her limited public engagement during her lifetime, Dickinson's work gained widespread recognition posthumously, cementing her status as a literary icon.

In the realm of science, Marie Curie stands out as a quiet revolutionary whose introverted qualities contributed to her extraordinary achievements. Curie's pioneering research on radioactivity earned her two Nobel Prizes, making her the first woman to receive this honor. Her preference for solitary, focused work allowed her to conduct meticulous experiments and make groundbreaking discoveries. Curie's dedication to her research often meant working long hours in isolation, but her perseverance and intellectual rigor led to significant advancements in science and medicine. Her legacy continues to inspire future generations of scientists, particularly women in STEM fields.

Another influential introvert is J.K. Rowling, the author of the Harry Potter series. Rowling's introverted nature and rich inner world fueled her creativity, allowing her to craft a detailed and imaginative universe that has captivated millions of readers worldwide. Her ability to immerse herself in her writing and develop complex characters and plots is a testament to the strengths of introversion. Despite facing numerous rejections early in her career, Rowling's quiet determination and belief in her work led to her eventual success, transforming her into one of the most successful and influential authors of our time.

Steve Wozniak, the co-founder of Apple Inc., exemplifies how introverts can revolutionize the world of technology. Wozniak's technical genius and passion for engineering were instrumental in developing the first personal computers. His preference for working behind the scenes, focusing on innovation and problem-solving, complemented the more extroverted and business-savvy approach of his co-founder, Steve Jobs. Together, their partnership created one of the most successful and influential technology companies in the world. Wozniak's story highlights how introverted qualities such as deep concentration and a love for tinkering can lead to groundbreaking technological advancements.

Rosa Parks, known as the "mother of the civil rights movement," was an introvert whose quiet strength and courage sparked significant social change. Parks' refusal to give up her seat on a segregated bus in Montgomery, Alabama, became a pivotal moment in the fight for racial equality. Her calm and resolute demeanor, coupled with her deep sense of justice, made her a powerful symbol of resistance against racial oppression. Parks' introverted nature did not prevent her from becoming a key figure in the civil rights movement; rather, it underscored the power of quiet, determined action in the face of injustice.

In the world of music, Freddie Mercury, the legendary frontman of Queen, was an introvert who captivated audiences with his extraordinary talent and charisma. Despite his flamboyant stage presence, Mercury was known to be shy and reserved offstage. His introverted nature allowed him to channel his emotions and creativity into his music, resulting in performances that were both electrifying and deeply personal. Mercury's ability to connect with audiences through his music, despite his introverted tendencies, demonstrates how introverts can use their inner depth to create powerful and lasting artistic expressions.

Bill Gates, the co-founder of Microsoft, is another example of an introverted revolutionary in the technology industry. Gates' introverted nature and analytical mind enabled him to focus on software development and strategic planning, leading to the creation of one of the most influential tech companies in the world. His preference for deep work and problem-solving, coupled with his visionary thinking, allowed him to foresee the potential of personal computing and drive the industry forward. Gates' success as an introverted leader underscores the importance of focus, perseverance, and strategic thinking in achieving revolutionary advancements.

The realm of visual arts has also been enriched by introverted revolutionaries like Vincent van Gogh. Van Gogh's introspective and solitary nature profoundly influenced his art, allowing him to explore and express his inner world through his paintings. Despite facing numerous personal struggles and societal challenges, van Gogh's dedication to his craft and his ability to convey deep emotions through his work have left an enduring impact on the art world. His story is a poignant reminder of how introverts can channel their inner experiences into creative expressions that resonate across time and culture.

Jane Austen, the renowned author of classic novels such as "Pride and Prejudice" and "Sense and Sensibility," was another introverted revolutionary in the literary world. Austen's keen observations of social dynamics and human behavior, coupled with her introspective nature, enabled her to create timeless works that continue to be celebrated for their wit, insight, and depth. Her preference for quiet, solitary writing allowed her to develop rich characters and intricate plots that explore the complexities of relationships and societal norms. Austen's legacy as a literary giant demonstrates how introverts can use their observational skills and introspection to produce works of profound impact and lasting value.

In the field of psychology, Carl Jung stands out as an introverted revolutionary whose theories have had a profound influence on our understanding of the human psyche. Jung's introspective nature and deep exploration of his own unconscious mind led to the development of concepts such as archetypes, the collective unconscious, and psychological types. His work has significantly shaped modern psychology and psychotherapy, providing valuable insights into the complexities of human behavior and personality. Jung's ability to delve into the depths of the mind and articulate his findings has had a lasting impact on the field, demonstrating the power of introverted introspection in advancing knowledge.

Chapter 16: Coping with Social Anxiety

Social anxiety can be a significant challenge for introverts, who often feel overwhelmed or uncomfortable in social situations. This discomfort arises from a deep-seated fear of being judged, embarrassed, or scrutinized by others. For introverts, who already prefer solitude and quiet environments, the pressure to navigate social interactions can exacerbate their anxiety. However, with the right strategies and coping mechanisms, introverts can manage their social anxiety and improve their confidence and comfort in social settings.

Understanding social anxiety is the first step towards managing it. Social anxiety is more than just shyness; it is a pervasive fear that affects many aspects of an individual's life. People with social anxiety often experience intense nervousness and self-consciousness in social situations, worrying excessively about being judged or humiliated. Physical symptoms such as sweating, trembling, rapid heartbeat, and even nausea can accompany these feelings. For introverts, who are already inclined to be more introspective and sensitive to external stimuli, these symptoms can be particularly pronounced. Recognizing the nature of social anxiety and acknowledging its impact is crucial for developing effective coping strategies.

One of the most effective ways for introverts to cope with social anxiety is through cognitive-behavioral therapy (CBT). CBT is a well-established therapeutic approach that focuses on identifying and challenging negative thought patterns and behaviors. For introverts with social anxiety, CBT can help reframe their perceptions of social situations and reduce the automatic negative thoughts that trigger anxiety. For instance, an introvert might fear that others are constantly judging them. Through CBT, they can learn to recognize this thought as a cognitive distortion and replace it with a more balanced perspective, such as understanding that most people are too focused on themselves to scrutinize others closely.

In addition to professional therapy, introverts can benefit from self-help techniques that align with CBT principles. One such technique is thought challenging, which involves examining the evidence for and against anxiety-provoking thoughts. For example, if an introvert believes they will embarrass themselves at a social event, they can list past experiences where this did not happen or where they handled the situation well. This exercise helps to weaken the power of negative thoughts and build confidence. Another technique is cognitive restructuring, which involves replacing negative thoughts with more positive or realistic ones. By practicing these techniques regularly, introverts can gradually shift their mindset and reduce their social anxiety.

Exposure therapy, a component of CBT, is another effective strategy for managing social anxiety. Exposure therapy involves gradually facing feared social situations in a controlled and systematic way, helping individuals build tolerance and reduce avoidance behaviors. For introverts, this might mean starting with less intimidating social interactions and gradually working up to more challenging ones. For instance, an introvert might begin by having brief conversations with coworkers or acquaintances and gradually progress to attending larger social gatherings or public speaking engagements. The key is to approach these situations with a sense of curiosity and openness, rather than fear and avoidance, and to celebrate small victories along the way.

Mindfulness and relaxation techniques can also play a significant role in helping introverts cope with social anxiety. Mindfulness involves paying attention to the present moment without judgment, which can help introverts manage their anxiety by grounding themselves in the here and now. Practices such as mindfulness meditation, deep breathing exercises, and progressive muscle relaxation can help reduce physical symptoms of anxiety and promote a sense of calm. For introverts, incorporating these practices into their daily routine can provide a valuable toolkit for managing stress and anxiety, both in and out of social situations.

Another important aspect of coping with social anxiety is building social skills and self-confidence. Introverts can benefit from learning and practicing specific social skills that can make interactions feel more manageable and less daunting. This might include developing active listening skills, which involve paying close attention to what others are saying and responding thoughtfully. It can also involve practicing conversation starters and learning how to navigate small talk, which can be particularly challenging for introverts. By improving their social skills, introverts can feel more equipped to handle social interactions and less anxious about making mistakes or being judged.

Developing a strong support network is also crucial for introverts coping with social anxiety. Having a few trusted friends or family members who understand and support their struggles can provide a valuable source of comfort and encouragement. These individuals can offer a safe space for introverts to express their feelings and practice social interactions without fear of judgment. Additionally, joining support groups, either in person or online, can connect introverts with others who share similar experiences and provide mutual support and understanding. Knowing that they are not alone in their struggles can be immensely reassuring and empowering for introverts with social anxiety.

Setting realistic goals and gradually increasing social exposure can also help introverts manage their anxiety. Rather than attempting to tackle large, intimidating social situations all at once, introverts can start with smaller, more manageable goals. For example, they might aim to attend a small gathering with close friends before attempting a larger social event. Gradually increasing their exposure to social situations allows introverts to build confidence and resilience at their own pace. It is important for introverts to be patient with themselves and recognize that progress may be slow and incremental, but every step forward is a positive achievement.

Self-care is another essential component of managing social anxiety for introverts. Taking time to recharge and engage in activities that bring joy and relaxation is crucial for maintaining mental and emotional well-being. This might include spending time in nature, pursuing hobbies and creative interests, or simply enjoying quiet moments of solitude. By prioritizing self-care, introverts can ensure that they have the energy and resilience needed to face social challenges. Additionally, practicing self-compassion and being kind to themselves when they experience anxiety can help introverts maintain a positive and supportive inner dialogue.

For introverts with social anxiety, it is also important to challenge societal expectations and norms that may contribute to their discomfort. Many cultures and societies place a high value on extroverted traits, such as sociability and assertiveness, which can make introverts feel inadequate or pressured to conform. By recognizing and challenging these societal biases, introverts can begin to embrace their own unique strengths and redefine success on their own terms. This might involve seeking out and connecting with introverted role models, reading books or articles that celebrate introversion, and finding ways to advocate for their needs in social and professional settings.

In addition to individual strategies, creating more inclusive environments that accommodate different personality types can help reduce social anxiety for introverts. In the workplace, for example, employers can promote a culture of respect for diverse working styles by providing options for quiet workspaces, flexible schedules, and opportunities for remote work. Encouraging a variety of communication methods, such as written correspondence and one-on-one meetings, can also help introverts feel more comfortable and confident in their interactions. In educational settings, teachers can create inclusive classrooms by offering a range of participation options, allowing students to contribute in ways that feel most comfortable for them.

Ultimately, coping with social anxiety requires a multifaceted approach that addresses both the internal and external factors that contribute to anxiety. For introverts, this means developing a deep understanding of their own needs and preferences, building practical skills and coping mechanisms, and seeking out supportive and inclusive environments. By combining cognitive-behavioral techniques, mindfulness practices, social skills training, and self-care strategies, introverts can gradually reduce their social anxiety and build a more confident and fulfilling social life.

Chapter 17: The Quiet Spectrum in Relationships

The quiet spectrum in relationships is a fascinating exploration of how introverts and extroverts navigate love and connection, often drawing on their unique strengths and facing distinctive challenges. This detailed examination delves into the dynamics of introverted relationships, the ways introverts form deep bonds, the potential for harmony and conflict with extroverted partners, and strategies for fostering fulfilling and balanced connections. Understanding the quiet spectrum in relationships is crucial for appreciating the diverse ways people experience and express love and connection.

At the heart of the quiet spectrum in relationships is the fundamental difference between introverted and extroverted personalities. Introverts typically find energy and solace in solitude and introspective activities, while extroverts gain energy from social interactions and external stimulation. These core differences can significantly influence how individuals approach relationships, communicate, and express affection. For introverts, relationships are often built on depth rather than breadth, with a preference for a few close, meaningful connections over a wide network of acquaintances. This inclination towards depth means that introverts are often highly selective about whom they allow into their inner circles, valuing authenticity, trust, and mutual understanding above all else.

In the context of romantic relationships, introverts tend to prioritize emotional intimacy and meaningful communication. They often seek partners who understand and respect their need for solitude and who can engage in deep, reflective conversations. Introverts may be less inclined to engage in constant social activities, preferring quiet, one-on-one time with their partners. This preference for intimate settings allows introverts to connect on a profound level, sharing their inner worlds and building strong, lasting bonds. For introverted couples, activities such as long walks, quiet dinners, or simply spending time together in silence can be deeply fulfilling.

One of the strengths of introverts in relationships is their ability to listen and empathize. Introverts often excel at providing thoughtful, attentive listening, which can make their partners feel heard and valued. This skill is particularly important in resolving conflicts and building trust, as introverts are likely to approach disagreements with a calm, reflective demeanor. By taking the time to understand their partner's perspective and expressing their own feelings with clarity and sensitivity, introverts can foster a sense of security and mutual respect in their relationships.

However, introverted relationships are not without their challenges. One of the primary difficulties introverts face is balancing their need for solitude with the demands of a romantic partnership. While introverts may deeply love and appreciate their partners, they also require regular alone time to recharge and reflect. This need for solitude can sometimes be misinterpreted by extroverted partners as a lack of interest or affection. It is crucial for introverts to communicate their needs clearly and for their partners to understand and respect these needs. Establishing boundaries and creating a routine that allows for both togetherness and alone time can help maintain a healthy balance.

In relationships where one partner is introverted and the other is extroverted, additional dynamics come into play. Extroverted partners may have different social needs and preferences, such as a desire for frequent social activities and larger social circles. These differences can lead to misunderstandings and conflicts if not addressed openly and with empathy. For example, an extroverted partner might feel neglected or frustrated if their introverted partner declines social invitations or prefers to stay in. Conversely, an introverted partner might feel overwhelmed or pressured by their extroverted partner's social demands.

Navigating these differences requires open communication and a willingness to compromise. Both partners need to understand and appreciate each other's needs and find ways to support each other. For instance, an introverted partner might agree to attend social events occasionally, while an extroverted partner might ensure that these events are balanced with quieter, more intimate activities. Finding common ground and creating shared experiences that both partners enjoy can help bridge the gap between their differing social preferences. It is also helpful for extroverted partners to seek out social interactions and activities independently, allowing their introverted partners the space they need without feeling deprived of social engagement.

Building a strong foundation of trust and mutual respect is essential for introverted-extroverted relationships. Trust allows both partners to feel secure in their relationship, even when they have different needs and preferences. This trust is built through consistent, honest communication and a genuine effort to understand and support each other. For introverts, expressing their love and appreciation in ways that resonate with their extroverted partners, such as through words of affirmation or acts of service, can help strengthen the bond. Similarly, extroverted partners can show their love by respecting their introverted partner's need for space and offering emotional support without being intrusive.

In addition to romantic relationships, the quiet spectrum also influences friendships and family connections. Introverted friendships often revolve around shared interests and deep, meaningful conversations. Introverts tend to form close-knit, loyal friendships with a few individuals rather than maintaining a large social network. These friendships are characterized by a high degree of trust, understanding, and emotional support. Introverts value friends who respect their need for solitude and who can engage in thoughtful, reflective discussions.

These friendships often provide a safe space for introverts to express their thoughts and feelings without fear of judgment.

Family relationships can be particularly challenging for introverts, especially in families with predominantly extroverted members. Family gatherings and social expectations can be overwhelming for introverts, who may feel pressured to participate in activities that drain their energy. It is important for introverted family members to communicate their needs and set boundaries, ensuring that they have the time and space to recharge. Family members can support introverts by being understanding and accommodating, such as providing quiet spaces during gatherings or allowing introverts to participate in activities at their own pace.

Another aspect of the quiet spectrum in relationships is the role of social media and digital communication. For introverts, online platforms can offer a way to connect with others on their terms, providing a sense of control and comfort. Introverts may prefer texting, emailing, or participating in online communities where they can engage in thoughtful, written communication rather than face-to-face interactions. Digital communication allows introverts to take their time in crafting responses and engaging with others, reducing the pressure and anxiety that can accompany real-time social interactions. However, it is important for introverts to balance online and offline interactions, ensuring that they maintain meaningful, in-person connections as well.

In professional relationships, introverts can leverage their strengths to build strong, collaborative connections. Introverts often excel in roles that require deep thinking, creativity, and attention to detail. By focusing on their strengths and finding ways to contribute meaningfully to their teams, introverts can build respect and trust among their colleagues. Effective communication is key, and introverts can benefit from finding their preferred modes of interaction, whether through written communication, one-on-one meetings, or small group discussions. Building a network of supportive colleagues who understand and appreciate their working style can help introverts thrive in professional settings.

For introverts, self-awareness and self-acceptance are critical components of building healthy relationships. Understanding their own needs, preferences, and boundaries allows introverts to communicate effectively and advocate for themselves. Self-acceptance involves recognizing and valuing their introverted traits, rather than viewing them as shortcomings. By embracing their introversion, introverts can approach relationships with confidence and authenticity, creating connections that are genuine and fulfilling.

Another important aspect of the quiet spectrum in relationships is the role of empathy and emotional intelligence. Introverts often have a high degree of empathy, which allows them to connect deeply with others and provide meaningful support. This empathy can be a powerful tool in relationships, helping introverts understand and respond to their partners' needs and emotions. Emotional intelligence, or the ability to recognize and manage one's own emotions and those of others, is also crucial for building and maintaining healthy relationships. By developing their emotional intelligence, introverts can navigate social interactions with greater ease and build stronger, more resilient connections.

Chapter 18: The Power of Listening

The power of listening is often understated, yet it holds immense value in various aspects of life, from personal relationships to professional settings. For introverts, listening is more than just a skill; it is a profound strength that defines their interactions and contributions. While introverts are frequently characterized by their preference for solitude and quiet environments, their ability to listen deeply and attentively stands out as a remarkable superpower.

Listening, at its core, is the ability to fully engage with and understand another person's communication. It goes beyond merely hearing words; it involves paying attention to the speaker's emotions, intentions, and non-verbal cues. Effective listening requires patience, empathy, and the willingness to put one's own thoughts aside temporarily to focus entirely on the speaker. For introverts, who often possess these qualities in abundance, listening becomes a natural and powerful tool for connection and understanding.

One of the key reasons introverts excel at listening is their preference for depth over breadth in their interactions. Unlike extroverts, who may thrive on engaging with many people and activities, introverts tend to seek out more meaningful, one-on-one conversations. This preference allows them to focus their attention more fully on the person they are interacting with, creating an environment where the speaker feels genuinely heard and understood. By concentrating on a few deep connections rather than numerous superficial ones, introverts can offer a level of attentiveness and empathy that is truly impactful.

In personal relationships, the power of listening manifests in the form of stronger, more intimate bonds. Introverts are often the confidants and trusted advisors among their friends and family, providing a safe space for others to share their thoughts and feelings. Their ability to listen without interrupting or judging allows people to express themselves openly and honestly. This non-judgmental listening fosters trust and emotional intimacy, as individuals feel validated and supported in their experiences. For introverts, the act of listening also serves as a way to connect with others on a deeper level, fulfilling their desire for meaningful relationships.

The benefits of listening extend beyond personal relationships into professional environments as well. In the workplace, effective listening can enhance teamwork, improve communication, and drive better decision-making. Introverts, with their natural inclination towards listening, can play a crucial role in fostering a collaborative and inclusive work culture. By actively listening to their colleagues, introverts can help ensure that all voices are heard, including those who may be less outspoken or more reserved. This inclusive approach not only promotes diversity of thought but also encourages a sense of belonging and respect among team members.

One specific area where introverts' listening skills shine is in leadership. Contrary to the traditional image of the extroverted, charismatic leader, introverts can be highly effective leaders by leveraging their listening abilities. Introverted leaders tend to be more approachable and empathetic, creating an environment where team members feel comfortable sharing their ideas and concerns. By listening carefully to their team, introverted leaders can gain valuable insights, build stronger relationships, and make informed decisions that reflect the collective input of their team. This leadership style, often referred to as servant leadership, emphasizes the importance of serving and supporting others, and it is a natural fit for introverts.

In addition to leadership, introverts' listening skills are invaluable in roles that require negotiation, mediation, and conflict resolution. Effective negotiation involves understanding the needs and perspectives of all parties involved, and introverts' ability to listen attentively can help uncover underlying issues and find common ground. In mediation and conflict resolution, the capacity to listen empathetically and without bias is essential for facilitating constructive dialogue and reaching mutually beneficial solutions. Introverts, with their calm and reflective demeanor, are often well-suited for these roles, as they can create a safe and respectful environment for open communication.

Listening also plays a critical role in creativity and problem-solving. By listening to diverse perspectives and ideas, introverts can gather a wealth of information and insights that fuel their creative thinking. This openness to different viewpoints allows introverts to see problems from multiple angles and develop innovative solutions. Additionally, the reflective nature of introverts means that they are more likely to take the time to fully process and synthesize information, leading to more thoughtful and well-considered outcomes.

Despite these strengths, introverts may face challenges in environments that prioritize speaking over listening. In many cultures and organizations, there is a tendency to value extroverted behaviors such as assertiveness and verbal communication. Introverts may feel pressure to conform to these norms, which can detract from their natural listening abilities. To counteract this, it is important to create environments that recognize and appreciate the value of listening. This can involve promoting a culture of active listening, where all team members are encouraged to listen attentively and respect different communication styles.

One way to foster a culture of listening is through training and development programs that emphasize the importance of effective communication. These programs can teach skills such as active listening, empathy, and reflective questioning, helping all team members improve their ability to listen and engage with others. Additionally, organizations can implement practices such as regular check-ins, feedback sessions, and collaborative meetings that prioritize listening and inclusive dialogue. By creating structures that support and reward listening, organizations can leverage the full potential of their introverted members and enhance overall communication and collaboration.

For introverts, developing their listening skills further can involve honing specific techniques and strategies. Active listening is one such technique, where the listener fully engages with the speaker, maintaining eye contact, nodding, and providing verbal affirmations. This approach not only shows that the listener is paying attention but also encourages the speaker to continue sharing. Reflective listening is another valuable technique, where the listener paraphrases or summarizes what the speaker has said to ensure understanding and demonstrate empathy. These techniques can help introverts enhance their listening abilities and create deeper connections with others.

Self-awareness is also crucial for introverts in maximizing their listening potential. Understanding their own strengths and limitations allows introverts to create conditions that support effective listening. This might involve managing their energy levels by scheduling quiet time for reflection or taking breaks during long meetings. By recognizing and addressing their own needs, introverts can maintain their focus and attentiveness, ensuring that they can listen effectively in various situations.

Chapter 19: Creativity and Introversion

Creativity and introversion are intimately linked in ways that are often overlooked or misunderstood. While the stereotypical image of a creative person might be someone who is exuberant, outgoing, and constantly interacting with others, introverts possess unique qualities that can foster profound creativity and innovation.

At the heart of the connection between creativity and introversion is the introvert's natural inclination towards introspection and solitude. Unlike extroverts, who derive energy from social interactions and external stimuli, introverts recharge and find inspiration in quiet, solitary environments. This preference for solitude allows introverts to delve deeply into their thoughts and ideas without the constant interruptions or distractions that can accompany social settings. The uninterrupted time alone provides fertile ground for the incubation of ideas and the deep reflection necessary for creative breakthroughs.

Introverts tend to be highly observant and detail-oriented, traits that are invaluable for creative endeavors. Their keen observational skills enable them to notice nuances and patterns that others might overlook, providing rich material for creative inspiration. This attention to detail can manifest in various forms, from the intricate descriptions in a piece of writing to the meticulous craftsmanship in a piece of art or the thoughtful design of a product. By taking the time to observe and reflect on the world around them, introverts can draw on a vast reservoir of insights and experiences that fuel their creativity.

One of the defining characteristics of introverts is their tendency towards deep thinking. Introverts often prefer to explore ideas and concepts thoroughly, examining them from multiple angles and considering their broader implications. This depth of thought is a significant asset for creative work, as it allows introverts to develop ideas that are well-considered, original, and impactful. Whether they are writing a novel, composing music, designing a new product, or solving a complex problem, introverts' ability to engage in sustained, focused thinking enables them to produce work of exceptional quality and depth.

Introverts are also often drawn to solitary activities that can enhance their creative skills. Reading, writing, drawing, and other solitary pursuits provide opportunities for introverts to hone their craft and develop their unique voice. These activities not only offer a means of self-expression but also serve as a way for introverts to process their thoughts and emotions. For example, keeping a journal can help introverts clarify their ideas and track their creative progress, while engaging in regular sketching or painting can improve their artistic abilities and provide a visual outlet for their imagination.

The creative process for introverts is often characterized by a period of intense focus and immersion. When introverts are engaged in a creative project, they can enter a state of flow, where they become completely absorbed in their work and lose track of time. This state of flow is conducive to creative productivity, as it allows introverts to work with a high degree of concentration and efficiency. By creating environments that support this level of focus, such as quiet workspaces or scheduled periods of uninterrupted time, introverts can maximize their creative output and achieve their full potential.

Despite their strengths, introverts may face challenges in environments that prioritize extroverted behaviors and collaborative work. Open-plan offices, frequent meetings, and group brainstorming sessions can be draining and disruptive for introverts, making it difficult for them to access their creative potential. To address these challenges, it is important to create work environments that respect and accommodate different working styles. This can involve providing options for remote work, offering quiet spaces for focused work, and allowing flexibility in how and when employees complete their tasks.

Collaboration, while often challenging for introverts, can also be a source of creative inspiration and growth. Introverts can benefit from collaborative work by leveraging their strengths in listening, empathy, and thoughtful contribution. In collaborative settings, introverts can play the role of synthesizers, bringing together diverse ideas and perspectives to create cohesive and innovative solutions. To make collaboration more introvert-friendly, teams can use techniques such as asynchronous brainstorming, where ideas are shared and developed individually before being discussed as a group. This approach allows introverts to contribute their ideas in a way that feels comfortable and aligns with their working style.

Another important aspect of nurturing creativity in introverts is the recognition and validation of their unique contributions. Introverts may be less likely to seek recognition or assert themselves in group settings, which can sometimes lead to their ideas being overlooked. By creating a culture that values and celebrates diverse contributions, organizations can ensure that introverts feel appreciated and motivated to share their creative insights. This can involve acknowledging individual achievements, providing opportunities for introverts to showcase their work, and encouraging a culture of respect and inclusivity.

Mentorship and support networks can also play a crucial role in helping introverts unleash their creative potential. Having a mentor who understands and values their strengths can provide introverts with the encouragement and guidance they need to navigate creative challenges and pursue their goals. Mentors can offer constructive feedback, share their own experiences, and help introverts build confidence in their abilities. Additionally, connecting with like-minded peers through creative communities or interest groups can provide introverts with a sense of belonging and support, fostering a collaborative and inspiring environment.

For introverts, self-awareness and self-care are essential components of nurturing creativity. Understanding their own needs, preferences, and rhythms allows introverts to create conditions that support their creative process. This might involve setting aside regular time for solitary activities, creating a dedicated workspace that minimizes distractions, or developing routines that incorporate periods of rest and reflection. By prioritizing self-care and respecting their own boundaries, introverts can maintain the energy and focus needed to sustain their creative endeavors.

The relationship between creativity and introversion is also influenced by the broader cultural and societal context. Societal norms and expectations can shape how introverts perceive their own creative abilities and how they are perceived by others. In cultures that prioritize extroverted traits such as assertiveness and sociability, introverts may feel pressure to conform and suppress their natural inclinations. To counteract this, it is important to promote a more inclusive and diverse understanding of creativity that recognizes and values different personality types and working styles. By challenging stereotypes and celebrating the contributions of introverts, we can create a more supportive environment for all individuals to express their creativity.

In educational settings, fostering creativity in introverted students involves creating a learning environment that accommodates different learning styles and encourages self-expression. Teachers can support introverted students by providing opportunities for independent work, offering quiet spaces for reflection, and using diverse teaching methods that cater to various preferences. Encouraging students to explore their interests and develop their unique talents can help introverted students build confidence and discover their creative potential. Additionally, promoting a culture of respect and inclusion in the classroom can ensure that all students feel valued and supported in their creative pursuits.

Chapter 20: Introverts and Social Media

The relationship between introverts and social media is multifaceted and complex, intertwining the allure of virtual interaction with the need for solitude and meaningful connection. Social media offers a platform where introverts can engage with others on their own terms, yet it also poses unique challenges that can disrupt their sense of balance and well-being.

Introverts often prefer deeper, one-on-one interactions to large group activities, and social media can cater to this preference by providing opportunities for more controlled and selective engagement. Platforms like Facebook, Twitter, Instagram, and LinkedIn allow introverts to connect with others without the immediate pressure of face-to-face interaction. This can be particularly beneficial for those who feel overwhelmed or drained by in-person socializing. Social media offers a space where introverts can reflect before responding, curate their interactions, and engage in meaningful conversations at their own pace.

One of the significant advantages of social media for introverts is the ability to build and maintain connections without the need for frequent in-person meetings. Introverts often cherish their alone time, and social media allows them to stay in touch with friends, family, and professional contacts while preserving their personal space. This balance between connection and solitude is crucial for their well-being, as it enables them to manage their social energy more effectively. Introverts can participate in social interactions when they feel ready and withdraw when they need to recharge, all within the digital realm.

Social media also serves as a platform for introverts to express themselves and share their thoughts, ideas, and creativity. Blogging, posting on social networks, and sharing multimedia content provide introverts with outlets to communicate and engage with a wider audience. These activities can be particularly empowering for introverts who may find it challenging to express themselves in traditional social settings. By sharing their passions and interests online, introverts can connect with like-minded individuals, find communities that resonate with them, and receive validation and support.

However, the benefits of social media are accompanied by several challenges that introverts must navigate. One of the primary concerns is the potential for social media to become overwhelming and draining. The constant influx of information, notifications, and social expectations can lead to cognitive overload and social fatigue. Introverts, who are already sensitive to excessive stimulation, may find it difficult to manage the demands of staying connected and keeping up with online interactions. This can result in feelings of anxiety, stress, and burnout.

Another challenge for introverts on social media is the pressure to present an idealized version of themselves. The curated nature of social media often emphasizes highlight reels and positive experiences, which can create unrealistic expectations and contribute to feelings of inadequacy. Introverts, who may already be prone to introspection and self-criticism, can find themselves comparing their lives to others and feeling that they fall short. This comparison can undermine their self-esteem and lead to a negative impact on their mental health.

The public nature of many social media interactions can also be daunting for introverts. Posting updates, photos, or opinions can expose introverts to scrutiny and judgment from a wide audience. This visibility can be intimidating and deter introverts from sharing their thoughts and experiences. Additionally, the potential for negative comments, trolling, and cyberbullying can create an environment of hostility that introverts may find particularly distressing. These challenges highlight the need for introverts to develop strategies for managing their social media use in a way that protects their well-being.

To find a healthy balance with social media, introverts can adopt several strategies that align with their natural preferences and strengths.

One effective approach is to set boundaries around social media use. This can involve limiting the amount of time spent on social platforms, scheduling specific times for checking and responding to messages, and turning off notifications to reduce interruptions. By establishing clear boundaries, introverts can prevent social media from encroaching on their personal time and space, allowing them to maintain a sense of control and balance.

Another important strategy is to curate their social media environment intentionally. Introverts can choose to follow accounts and join groups that align with their interests and values, creating a positive and supportive online community. They can also unfollow or mute accounts that contribute to stress, negativity, or comparison. By curating their social media feeds, introverts can create a digital space that feels nurturing and aligned with their needs.

Mindful social media use is another key practice for introverts. This involves being intentional and conscious about how and why they engage with social media. Introverts can reflect on their motivations for using social media and assess whether it aligns with their goals and values. They can also practice mindful scrolling, where they pay attention to their emotional responses and take breaks if they feel overwhelmed or distressed. Mindful social media use encourages introverts to engage with digital content in a way that feels meaningful and fulfilling.

Introverts can also leverage social media as a tool for personal growth and learning. Many platforms offer access to educational resources, professional networks, and opportunities for skill development. By focusing on these aspects, introverts can use social media to enhance their knowledge, advance their careers, and connect with mentors and peers in their field. This purposeful use of social media can provide a sense of accomplishment and enrichment, counterbalancing the potential downsides of online engagement.

Maintaining a balance between online and offline activities is crucial for introverts. While social media can offer valuable connections and opportunities, it is important for introverts to prioritize real-world interactions and experiences. Engaging in offline hobbies, spending time in nature, and cultivating face-to-face relationships can provide a grounding counterpoint to the digital world. By striking a balance between online and offline life, introverts can ensure that their social media use enhances rather than detracts from their overall well-being.

Self-care practices are essential for introverts to manage the impact of social media. Regularly engaging in activities that promote relaxation and rejuvenation, such as meditation, exercise, reading, or creative pursuits, can help introverts recharge and maintain their emotional equilibrium. Self-care also involves recognizing when social media use is becoming detrimental and taking steps to address it, such as taking digital detoxes or seeking support from friends, family, or mental health professionals.

Ultimately, finding balance with social media requires introverts to be attuned to their own needs and preferences. Each individual may have different thresholds for social interaction and different ways of engaging with digital content. By experimenting with various strategies and paying attention to their emotional and mental responses, introverts can develop a personalized approach to social media that supports their well-being and creativity.

Chapter 21: The Introverted Entrepreneur

The concept of the introverted entrepreneur might initially seem paradoxical to many, given the stereotypical image of entrepreneurs as outgoing, charismatic, and highly sociable individuals who thrive on networking and public speaking. However, this narrow perspective fails to acknowledge the unique strengths and capabilities that introverts bring to the entrepreneurial landscape. Introverts, often characterized by their preference for solitary activities, deep thinking, and reflective nature, can indeed excel in building successful businesses, often in ways that align with their intrinsic qualities and personal values.

One of the key strengths of introverted entrepreneurs lies in their ability to focus intensely on their work. Unlike their extroverted counterparts who may seek constant social interaction and external stimulation, introverts often find solitude to be a fertile ground for creativity and innovation. This ability to concentrate deeply can lead to the development of unique ideas and solutions that might not emerge in a more distracted, social environment. Introverts tend to think things through thoroughly before acting, which can result in well-considered business strategies and decisions. This meticulous approach to planning and problem-solving can be a significant advantage in the competitive world of entrepreneurship.

Moreover, introverts often excel at listening, a skill that is invaluable in business. Effective communication is not just about speaking well, but also about understanding the needs, desires, and concerns of clients, customers, and employees. Introverted entrepreneurs typically possess the patience and attentiveness required to truly hear what others are saying. This can foster stronger relationships and build trust, which are critical components of a successful business. By listening carefully, introverts can gather valuable insights that can inform their business strategies and help them create products or services that better meet the needs of their target market.

In addition to their listening skills, introverts often have a natural inclination towards empathy. They are usually more attuned to the emotions and experiences of others, which can translate into a deeper understanding of their customers' needs. This empathetic approach can be a powerful tool in customer service and marketing, enabling introverted entrepreneurs to connect with their audience on a more personal level. By creating a business that genuinely cares about its customers, introverts can cultivate a loyal and dedicated customer base.

Introverts are also known for their strong preference for meaningful, one-on-one interactions over superficial networking. This can actually work to their advantage in the business world. While large networking events and social gatherings may be daunting, introverts often thrive in smaller, more intimate settings where they can build deeper, more meaningful connections. These close-knit relationships can lead to more substantial and lasting business partnerships, mentorships, and collaborations. By focusing on quality over quantity in their professional relationships, introverted entrepreneurs can create a solid support network that provides valuable guidance and resources.

Another notable strength of introverted entrepreneurs is their ability to lead by example. Introverts often lead through actions rather than words, demonstrating a strong work ethic, integrity, and dedication. This type of leadership can inspire and motivate employees, creating a positive and productive work environment. Introverted leaders are often perceived as more approachable and trustworthy, which can foster a sense of loyalty and commitment among their team members. By leading with humility and authenticity, introverts can cultivate a company culture that values respect, collaboration, and mutual support.

Furthermore, introverts' natural inclination towards introspection can drive continuous personal and professional growth. They often spend time reflecting on their experiences, analyzing their strengths and weaknesses, and seeking ways to improve. This commitment to self-improvement can lead to significant advancements in their business skills and acumen over time. Introverted entrepreneurs are usually lifelong learners, always seeking new knowledge and insights that can help them stay ahead in their industry. Their reflective nature allows them to adapt and evolve their business strategies in response to changing market conditions and emerging trends.

While the traditional entrepreneurial path may emphasize extroverted activities such as pitching to investors, attending networking events, and making public presentations, introverted entrepreneurs can build their businesses in ways that play to their strengths. For instance, they can leverage digital platforms and online communities to connect with others, share their ideas, and promote their business. Social media, blogs, podcasts, and webinars provide opportunities for introverts to reach a broad audience without the need for face-to-face interactions. By using these tools, introverted entrepreneurs can effectively market their products or services while staying within their comfort zone.

Additionally, introverted entrepreneurs can delegate tasks that do not align with their strengths. By hiring or collaborating with individuals who excel in areas such as sales, marketing, or public relations, introverts can focus on the aspects of the business that they are most passionate about and proficient in. This strategic delegation not only enhances the overall performance of the business but also allows introverted entrepreneurs to maintain their energy and avoid burnout.

Chapter 22: Mindfulness and Introversion

Mindfulness and introversion are two concepts that naturally complement each other, creating a powerful synergy for cultivating inner peace and overall well-being. Introverts, characterized by their preference for solitude and deep reflection, often find mindfulness practices to be particularly beneficial in navigating their internal world and enhancing their sense of calm and contentment. By integrating mindfulness into their daily lives, introverts can develop a greater awareness of their thoughts, emotions, and surroundings, fostering a deeper connection with themselves and a more profound sense of inner peace.

At its core, mindfulness is the practice of paying attention to the present moment with an open, non-judgmental attitude. This involves being fully aware of one's thoughts, feelings, bodily sensations, and environment without becoming overly reactive or overwhelmed. For introverts, who naturally gravitate towards introspection and self-reflection, mindfulness can serve as an invaluable tool for managing stress, anxiety, and other negative emotions. By cultivating a mindful awareness of their inner experiences, introverts can learn to observe their thoughts and feelings without becoming entangled in them, allowing for a greater sense of emotional balance and stability.

One of the primary benefits of mindfulness for introverts is its ability to reduce stress and promote relaxation. Introverts often experience stress in social situations or environments that are overly stimulating. Mindfulness techniques, such as deep breathing exercises, meditation, and progressive muscle relaxation, can help introverts to calm their nervous system and reduce the physical and mental symptoms of stress. By regularly practicing these techniques, introverts can create a sense of inner tranquility that enables them to navigate challenging situations with greater ease and composure.

Moreover, mindfulness can enhance an introvert's capacity for self-awareness and self-acceptance. Introverts tend to spend a significant amount of time in self-reflection, which can sometimes lead to overthinking or self-criticism. Mindfulness encourages a gentle, non-judgmental awareness of one's thoughts and feelings, promoting a more compassionate and accepting attitude towards oneself. This shift in perspective can help introverts to let go of self-critical thoughts and develop a healthier, more positive self-image. By embracing their true selves and recognizing their inherent worth, introverts can cultivate a deeper sense of inner peace and self-confidence.

Another important aspect of mindfulness for introverts is its potential to enhance their relationships with others. While introverts may prefer solitude, meaningful connections with others are still essential for their well-being. Mindfulness can improve interpersonal relationships by fostering greater empathy, patience, and understanding. By being fully present and attentive in their interactions, introverts can create deeper, more authentic connections with others. This mindful presence allows them to listen more effectively, respond with greater empathy, and build stronger, more fulfilling relationships.

In addition to its benefits for emotional and relational well-being, mindfulness can also enhance cognitive functioning and creativity. Introverts often excel in activities that require deep thinking and creativity, such as writing, art, and problem-solving. Mindfulness practices, such as focused attention meditation and mindful observation, can improve concentration, enhance memory, and stimulate creative thinking. By quieting the mind and reducing distractions, introverts can tap into their innate creativity and generate innovative ideas and solutions. This heightened cognitive clarity and creative potential can be particularly beneficial in both personal and professional endeavors.

Mindfulness can also support introverts in managing social anxiety and enhancing their social skills. Many introverts experience anxiety in social situations, which can limit their ability to fully engage and connect with others. Mindfulness-based interventions, such as mindful exposure and social mindfulness practices, can help introverts to gradually reduce their social anxiety and build confidence in their social interactions. By practicing mindfulness in social settings, introverts can learn to stay grounded, present, and authentic, allowing them to engage more comfortably and genuinely with others.

Furthermore, mindfulness can help introverts to develop a greater sense of purpose and meaning in their lives. Introverts often seek deeper meaning and fulfillment in their experiences, and mindfulness can facilitate this quest by encouraging a deeper exploration of one's values, passions, and goals. Through practices such as mindful journaling, values clarification, and purpose meditation, introverts can gain clarity about what truly matters to them and align their actions with their core values. This alignment can foster a profound sense of purpose and direction, contributing to overall life satisfaction and inner peace.

In the context of daily life, there are numerous practical ways that introverts can incorporate mindfulness into their routines. One simple yet effective practice is mindful breathing. By taking a few moments each day to focus on their breath, introverts can anchor themselves in the present moment and create a sense of calm and clarity. Another practice is mindful walking, which involves paying close attention to the sensations of walking and the environment around them. This can be a particularly grounding activity for introverts, who often enjoy solitary walks in nature.

Mindful eating is another practice that can benefit introverts by promoting a greater awareness of their body's needs and fostering a healthier relationship with food. By eating slowly and savoring each bite, introverts can tune into their hunger and fullness cues, appreciate the sensory experience of eating, and develop a more mindful approach to nourishment.

Additionally, mindfulness meditation is a cornerstone practice that can significantly benefit introverts. Setting aside time each day for meditation allows introverts to cultivate a deeper sense of inner peace, clarity, and emotional regulation. Whether through guided meditations, body scan practices, or loving-kindness meditations, introverts can explore different forms of mindfulness meditation to find what resonates best with them.

Another valuable practice is mindful journaling, which involves writing about one's thoughts, feelings, and experiences with a mindful attitude. This practice can help introverts to process their emotions, gain insights into their inner world, and develop a greater sense of self-awareness and self-compassion. By regularly engaging in mindful journaling, introverts can create a safe space for reflection and personal growth.

For introverts who enjoy creative activities, mindful art practices such as drawing, painting, or crafting can be particularly therapeutic. By immersing themselves fully in the creative process, introverts can experience a state of flow and mindfulness that enhances their sense of well-being and inner peace.

Finally, practicing mindfulness in daily activities, such as mindful listening, mindful communication, and mindful work, can help introverts to bring a sense of presence and intention to every aspect of their lives. By approaching each task with mindful awareness, introverts can enhance their productivity, reduce stress, and create a more balanced and fulfilling life.

Chapter 23: The Introvert's Guide to Networking

Networking can often feel daunting for introverts, who generally prefer intimate settings and deep, meaningful conversations over large social gatherings and superficial interactions. However, networking is an essential aspect of both personal and professional growth. For introverts, approaching networking in a way that leverages their strengths can transform it from a dreaded task into a rewarding experience. By understanding their unique qualities and adopting strategies that align with their preferences, introverts can build a robust and supportive network without compromising their comfort or authenticity.

One of the first steps for introverts to succeed in networking is to reframe their perspective on what networking actually entails. Rather than viewing it as a superficial exchange of business cards or forced small talk, introverts can see networking as an opportunity to build genuine relationships based on mutual interests and values. This shift in mindset can make the process feel more authentic and less intimidating. Introverts excel at creating deep connections, so focusing on the quality of interactions rather than the quantity can make networking more manageable and meaningful.

Preparation is another key factor for introverts in successful networking. Introverts often feel more comfortable and confident when they are well-prepared. Before attending a networking event or meeting, they can research the attendees, speakers, or topics of discussion. This preparation allows them to identify common interests and potential conversation starters, making it easier to initiate and sustain meaningful interactions. Additionally, setting specific goals for networking events, such as aiming to connect with a certain number of people or to learn about a particular industry, can provide a sense of direction and purpose.

Small, intimate gatherings are often more conducive to meaningful networking for introverts than large, crowded events. Introverts can seek out or create opportunities for smaller group interactions, such as attending workshops, seminars, or industry-specific meetups where they can engage in deeper discussions with like-minded individuals. Hosting their own small networking events or dinners can also be an effective way for introverts to connect with others in a comfortable and controlled environment. By choosing settings that align with their preferences, introverts can make networking a more enjoyable and productive experience.

Another effective strategy for introverts is to leverage one-on-one interactions. Introverts often thrive in one-on-one settings where they can have in-depth conversations without the distractions of a large group. They can arrange coffee meetings, lunches, or video calls with individuals they want to connect with, allowing for a more personal and meaningful exchange. Following up with individuals they meet at larger events through personalized messages or invitations for one-on-one meetings can also help to build and strengthen relationships over time.

Listening is a natural strength for introverts, and it can be a powerful tool in networking. By actively listening to others, introverts can demonstrate genuine interest and empathy, which helps to build trust and rapport. Good listening also enables introverts to understand the needs, interests, and challenges of others, providing valuable insights that can inform future interactions and collaborations. This focus on listening rather than dominating conversations can make introverts more memorable and appreciated by their networking contacts.

In addition to listening, asking thoughtful questions is another way introverts can excel in networking. Introverts can use their curiosity and reflective nature to ask open-ended questions that encourage deeper discussions. Questions about someone's background, interests, current projects, or future goals can lead to meaningful exchanges and reveal common ground. This approach not only helps introverts to navigate conversations more comfortably but also shows their conversational partners that they are genuinely interested in them as individuals.

Introverts can also benefit from leveraging online networking platforms, which can provide a less intimidating and more flexible way to connect with others. Platforms such as LinkedIn, industry-specific forums, and social media groups offer opportunities to engage with professionals, share insights, and build relationships without the pressure of face-to-face interactions. Introverts can participate in online discussions, join virtual events, and connect with individuals through personalized messages. These online interactions can serve as a foundation for future in-person meetings, making them feel more familiar and less daunting.

Follow-up is an essential aspect of effective networking, and it plays to the strengths of introverts who often excel at thoughtful communication. After meeting someone, introverts can send a personalized follow-up message to express their appreciation for the conversation, share relevant information or resources, and suggest a future meeting or collaboration. This proactive approach helps to reinforce the connection and keeps the relationship moving forward. Handwritten notes or personalized emails can leave a lasting impression and show that the introvert values the relationship.

Introverts should also be mindful of managing their energy levels when networking. Networking events can be draining, so it's important for introverts to take care of themselves and set boundaries to avoid burnout. This might involve scheduling downtime before and after events, taking breaks during the event to recharge, and not overcommitting to multiple events in a short period. By prioritizing self-care and recognizing their own limits, introverts can maintain their well-being while still engaging in effective networking.

Another valuable strategy for introverts is to partner with an extroverted colleague or friend when attending networking events. Extroverted partners can help to initiate conversations and introduce introverts to new contacts, easing the pressure of starting interactions. This dynamic can allow introverts to contribute meaningfully to conversations without feeling overwhelmed by the need to constantly initiate. Additionally, observing how extroverted partners navigate social interactions can provide introverts with useful insights and techniques that they can adapt to their own style.

Building a personal brand is another way introverts can enhance their networking efforts. By establishing themselves as knowledgeable and trustworthy in their field, introverts can attract like-minded individuals and opportunities. This can be achieved through writing articles or blogs, speaking at small events, sharing insights on social media, or participating in industry panels. A strong personal brand can serve as a conversation starter and provide a sense of credibility that makes networking interactions smoother and more impactful.

Volunteering for roles within professional organizations or community groups can also be a strategic way for introverts to network. By taking on responsibilities such as organizing events, managing projects, or contributing to group activities, introverts can demonstrate their skills and dedication while naturally building relationships with others. These roles often provide structured and purposeful interactions that can feel more comfortable and meaningful than casual networking.

Mentorship is another avenue through which introverts can expand their network. Seeking out mentors who can provide guidance, support, and introductions to other professionals can be invaluable. Additionally, offering to mentor others can help introverts to establish themselves as knowledgeable and approachable, creating opportunities for reciprocal learning and networking. Mentorship relationships are typically based on trust and mutual respect, making them well-suited to the strengths of introverts.

Introverts should also remember that networking is a long-term process rather than a one-time event. Building a network takes time, and it's important to nurture relationships consistently. Regularly checking in with contacts, offering support or resources, and staying engaged in professional communities can help introverts to maintain and grow their network over time. This steady, thoughtful approach aligns well with the introverted preference for deep, lasting connections.

Chapter 24: Quiet Activism

Quiet activism is a powerful yet often understated approach to making a difference in the world. It embodies the idea that significant change does not always require loud, public displays of protest or outspoken advocacy. Instead, it emphasizes subtle, thoughtful actions that can collectively lead to substantial and meaningful progress. This form of activism is particularly well-suited to introverts, who may feel uncomfortable with traditional, high-energy forms of activism. By leveraging their strengths—such as deep reflection, empathy, and a preference for one-on-one or small group interactions—quiet activists can effect change in a manner that is authentic to them and sustainable over the long term.

One of the core tenets of quiet activism is the belief in the power of small, consistent actions. While large-scale movements and demonstrations often capture public attention, it is the everyday actions of individuals that can create lasting impact. Quiet activists understand that change often begins at the personal level and that by embodying the values they wish to promote, they can influence those around them in meaningful ways. This might include making conscious choices about how they live their lives, such as adopting environmentally sustainable practices, supporting ethical businesses, or advocating for social justice through their purchasing decisions.

Moreover, quiet activists often focus on creating change within their immediate communities. They recognize that local actions can have a ripple effect, spreading outward to influence broader societal norms and policies. By engaging in community-based initiatives, introverts can build strong, trust-based relationships that enable them to collaborate effectively with others. This might involve volunteering for local organizations, participating in community gardens, organizing neighborhood cleanups, or supporting local artisans and businesses. Through these activities, quiet activists can demonstrate their commitment to their values and inspire others to take similar actions.

Education is another powerful tool for quiet activism. Introverts often excel at deep, reflective thinking and have a natural inclination towards learning and sharing knowledge. Quiet activists can leverage this strength by educating themselves about the issues they care about and then sharing this knowledge with others in thoughtful, non-confrontational ways. This might involve writing articles, creating informative social media content, or hosting small discussion groups. By providing well-researched information and fostering open dialogue, quiet activists can help to raise awareness and encourage others to think critically about important issues.

In addition to direct actions and education, quiet activism often involves supporting and amplifying the voices of others. Introverts may not always feel comfortable being in the spotlight, but they can use their platforms and resources to elevate the work of more outspoken activists. This might include sharing the work of others on social media, providing financial support to activist organizations, or using their professional skills to assist with behind-the-scenes efforts such as organizing events, managing communications, or designing promotional materials. By contributing in these ways, quiet activists can play a crucial role in the success of larger movements without needing to take center stage.

Storytelling is another effective strategy for quiet activism. Introverts often have a gift for listening and empathy, which enables them to understand and convey the experiences of others in a compelling and sensitive manner. By sharing personal stories or the stories of those affected by the issues they care about, quiet activists can humanize abstract problems and foster a deeper emotional connection with their audience. This can be done through writing, photography, film, or other creative mediums. By highlighting individual experiences and struggles, quiet activists can inspire empathy and action in others.

Quiet activists also place a strong emphasis on building relationships and networks. They understand that lasting change is often driven by strong, supportive communities. By cultivating deep, meaningful connections with others who share their values, quiet activists can create a network of mutual support and collaboration. These relationships provide a foundation for collective action and enable quiet activists to pool their resources and expertise to tackle larger challenges. This might involve forming or joining local advocacy groups, participating in online forums, or attending small, focused gatherings where they can connect with like-minded individuals.

Another important aspect of quiet activism is self-care and sustainability. Introverts often need time alone to recharge, and this need can sometimes be at odds with the demands of traditional activism. Quiet activists recognize the importance of balancing their activism with self-care to avoid burnout and maintain their effectiveness over the long term. This might involve setting boundaries around their involvement in activist activities, taking regular breaks, and engaging in restorative practices such as meditation, nature walks, or creative pursuits. By prioritizing their well-being, quiet activists can sustain their commitment to their causes and continue to contribute meaningfully over time.

Quiet activism also involves a strategic and long-term approach to change. Introverts often excel at planning and thinking ahead, which can be a significant advantage in activism. Quiet activists can use their strategic thinking skills to identify key leverage points where their efforts can have the greatest impact. This might involve focusing on specific policy changes, supporting long-term initiatives, or working to shift cultural attitudes and norms. By taking a thoughtful and deliberate approach, quiet activists can maximize the effectiveness of their actions and contribute to lasting change.

One of the most powerful aspects of quiet activism is its potential to create change through example. By living their values authentically and consistently, quiet activists can inspire others to do the same. This might involve demonstrating a commitment to sustainability, showing kindness and compassion in their interactions, or standing up for justice in their daily lives. Through their actions, quiet activists can model the behavior they wish to see in the world, encouraging others to follow suit.

Moreover, quiet activism is often about patience and persistence. Social change rarely happens overnight, and it requires sustained effort and dedication. Quiet activists understand that their contributions, no matter how small they may seem, are part of a larger tapestry of efforts working towards a common goal. By remaining committed to their values and continuing to take action, quiet activists can contribute to the slow but steady progress that leads to meaningful change.

Chapter 25: The Emotional Landscape of Introverts

The emotional landscape of introverts is a rich and intricate tapestry, characterized by a depth of feeling and a nuanced understanding of both their own emotions and those of others. Introverts are often portrayed as quiet and reserved, but beneath this exterior lies a complex inner world where emotions are deeply felt and thoughtfully processed. Understanding the emotional experiences of introverts involves exploring how they perceive, manage, and express their feelings, and how these processes are influenced by their introverted nature.

At the heart of the introverted emotional experience is a heightened sensitivity to internal and external stimuli. Introverts are naturally inclined to turn inward, reflecting deeply on their thoughts and feelings. This introspective tendency allows them to develop a profound self-awareness and an acute sensitivity to the subtleties of their emotional states. Unlike extroverts, who may seek external stimulation to feel energized, introverts often find that their energy is replenished through solitude and quiet contemplation. This introspection is a double-edged sword: it enables a deep understanding of oneself, but it can also lead to overthinking and a tendency to dwell on negative emotions.

One of the defining characteristics of the emotional landscape of introverts is their ability to experience emotions intensely. While they may not always outwardly express their feelings, introverts often feel emotions more deeply and profoundly than their extroverted counterparts. This intensity can make introverts particularly empathetic and compassionate, as they are able to connect with and understand the emotions of others on a deep level. However, it can also make them more susceptible to emotional overwhelm, especially in environments that are overly stimulating or demanding.

Introverts often have a rich inner life, where they spend considerable time reflecting on their experiences, analyzing their emotions, and making sense of the world around them. This inner dialogue is a key aspect of their emotional processing. By turning inward, introverts can gain insights into their feelings, identify the root causes of their emotions, and develop strategies for managing them. This reflective process can be incredibly therapeutic, allowing introverts to navigate their emotional landscape with greater clarity and understanding.

However, this introspective nature can also present challenges. Introverts may find themselves caught in a cycle of rumination, where they repeatedly analyze and rehash their thoughts and feelings. This can lead to heightened anxiety and a tendency to fixate on negative experiences. It is important for introverts to develop healthy coping mechanisms to manage this tendency, such as mindfulness practices, journaling, or engaging in creative activities that allow them to channel their emotions in a constructive way.

Another important aspect of the emotional landscape of introverts is their preference for deep, meaningful connections. Introverts often seek out relationships that are built on trust, understanding, and mutual respect. They value quality over quantity when it comes to social interactions and are more likely to invest their time and energy in a few close relationships rather than a wide network of acquaintances. This preference for depth in relationships allows introverts to form strong emotional bonds and experience a sense of security and support.

In their interactions with others, introverts often exhibit a high degree of empathy and emotional intelligence. They are skilled at picking up on subtle emotional cues and are often attuned to the unspoken feelings of those around them. This ability to understand and empathize with others can make introverts excellent listeners and supportive friends. However, it can also be emotionally draining, as introverts may absorb and internalize the emotions of others, leading to emotional fatigue.

The way introverts express their emotions can also be influenced by their introverted nature. While they may feel emotions intensely, they are often more reserved in expressing them outwardly. This can be misunderstood by others as a lack of emotion or indifference, but in reality, introverts may simply prefer to process their feelings privately. They may express their emotions through creative outlets, such as writing, art, or music, where they can channel their inner experiences into tangible forms of expression.

In romantic relationships, introverts often bring a depth of feeling and a capacity for intimacy that can be incredibly rewarding. They tend to be loyal, attentive partners who value deep emotional connections. However, they may also need more alone time than their extroverted counterparts, which can sometimes be misunderstood as a lack of interest or affection. Clear communication and mutual understanding are crucial in ensuring that the emotional needs of both partners are met.

In the workplace, introverts may experience a different set of emotional challenges and strengths. They often thrive in roles that allow for independent work and deep concentration, where they can apply their reflective nature and attention to detail. However, introverts may find high-energy, social work environments to be draining and may struggle with activities that require constant social interaction, such as networking events or team-building exercises. It is important for introverts to find a balance that allows them to utilize their strengths while also managing their energy levels and emotional well-being.

Managing stress and emotional well-being is a critical aspect of navigating the emotional landscape of introverts. Introverts may be more prone to stress and anxiety, particularly in environments that are overly stimulating or demanding. Developing a toolkit of stress management techniques can be invaluable in maintaining emotional balance. This might include practices such as mindfulness meditation, yoga, spending time in nature, or engaging in hobbies that bring joy and relaxation. Establishing boundaries and prioritizing self-care are also essential in preventing burnout and maintaining emotional health.

One of the most important aspects of understanding the emotional landscape of introverts is recognizing the value of solitude. For introverts, alone time is not just a preference; it is a necessity for emotional well-being. Solitude provides a space for introverts to recharge, reflect, and process their emotions without the distractions and demands of social interactions. Embracing solitude can be a powerful way for introverts to cultivate a sense of inner peace and emotional resilience.

The role of solitude in the emotional lives of introverts cannot be overstated. It is during these quiet moments that introverts can engage in self-reflection, explore their inner thoughts and feelings, and gain a deeper understanding of themselves. This process of introspection allows introverts to identify their emotional needs, set personal goals, and develop a sense of purpose and direction. By embracing solitude as a valuable and necessary part of their lives, introverts can enhance their emotional well-being and foster a greater sense of self-awareness and self-acceptance.

In addition to solitude, introverts often benefit from engaging in creative and expressive activities that allow them to channel their emotions in constructive ways. Creative outlets such as writing, painting, music, or crafting can provide a therapeutic space for introverts to explore and express their inner experiences. These activities not only offer a means of emotional expression but also contribute to a sense of fulfillment and joy. By nurturing their creative passions, introverts can enhance their emotional well-being and cultivate a sense of purpose and meaning.

The emotional landscape of introverts is also shaped by their sensitivity to the environment around them. Introverts often have a heightened awareness of sensory stimuli, such as noise, light, and social dynamics. This sensitivity can make certain environments, such as crowded or noisy spaces, particularly overwhelming. Creating a calming and supportive environment can be essential for introverts to maintain their emotional balance. This might involve designing a personal space that is quiet, comfortable, and conducive to relaxation and reflection. Incorporating elements such as soft lighting, soothing colors, and natural materials can create a sanctuary where introverts can recharge and find solace.

Supportive relationships play a crucial role in the emotional lives of introverts. While they may need ample alone time, introverts also value deep, meaningful connections with others. Having a trusted support network of friends, family, or colleagues who understand and respect their needs can provide a sense of security and belonging. These relationships offer a space for introverts to share their thoughts and feelings, seek guidance and support, and engage in mutually fulfilling interactions. Building and maintaining these supportive relationships requires clear communication, mutual respect, and a shared understanding of each other's emotional needs.

Chapter 26: The Health of Introverts

The health of introverts, encompassing both mental and physical wellbeing, is a multifaceted subject that requires a nuanced understanding of their unique needs and characteristics. Introverts, who often thrive in environments that allow for solitude and deep thought, face specific challenges and opportunities in maintaining their overall health.

Introverts are typically characterized by their preference for solitude, introspection, and a lower threshold for stimulation compared to extroverts. These traits can significantly influence their mental health. On the one hand, introverts often have rich inner lives and can derive a great deal of satisfaction from solitary activities such as reading, writing, and creative pursuits. This ability to find contentment in solitude can serve as a protective factor for mental health, providing introverts with a reliable source of pleasure and fulfillment.

However, introverts can also face mental health challenges that stem from societal expectations and the need to navigate an often extrovert-dominated world. Many social, educational, and professional environments are designed with extroverted traits in mind, such as group work, frequent social interactions, and open-plan workspaces. These settings can be overwhelming and draining for introverts, leading to stress and anxiety. The pressure to conform to extroverted norms can result in feelings of inadequacy or the perception that their natural inclinations are less valued or appreciated.

One of the key mental health concerns for introverts is social anxiety. While not all introverts experience social anxiety, they are more prone to it due to their sensitivity to social stimulation and their preference for controlled, predictable interactions. Social anxiety can manifest as intense fear or discomfort in social situations, leading to avoidance behaviors that can further isolate the individual and exacerbate feelings of loneliness and distress. Addressing social anxiety requires a combination of strategies, including cognitive-behavioral therapy (CBT), mindfulness practices, and gradual exposure to social situations in a way that feels manageable and safe.

Introverts are also at risk of experiencing burnout, particularly when they are forced to engage in prolonged social interaction or high-stimulation environments without adequate opportunities for rest and recovery. Burnout is characterized by emotional, mental, and physical exhaustion, often accompanied by feelings of cynicism and a sense of inefficacy. For introverts, preventing burnout involves recognizing their limits, setting boundaries, and ensuring they have sufficient time for solitude and recharging.

Depression is another mental health issue that can affect introverts, particularly if they experience chronic stress, social isolation, or feelings of being misunderstood. Introverts may be more inclined to internalize their emotions and ruminate on negative thoughts, which can contribute to depressive symptoms. It is crucial for introverts to have access to supportive relationships and mental health resources that validate their experiences and provide appropriate interventions, such as therapy and medication when needed.

In terms of physical health, introverts may experience unique challenges related to their lifestyle and coping mechanisms. For instance, introverts who spend a significant amount of time alone may be less likely to engage in physical activities or group exercises, which can impact their overall physical fitness and health. Sedentary behaviors, combined with potential stress-related eating habits, can increase the risk of chronic conditions such as obesity, cardiovascular disease, and diabetes. Therefore, it is important for introverts to find physical activities that they enjoy and can engage in on their own or in low-stimulation environments, such as walking, yoga, swimming, or solo sports.

Sleep is another critical aspect of physical health that can be influenced by introversion. Introverts may have a heightened need for quality sleep to recover from the mental and emotional demands of social interactions. Poor sleep hygiene, including irregular sleep schedules and the use of electronic devices before bedtime, can negatively impact sleep quality and duration. Establishing a consistent sleep routine, creating a calming bedtime environment, and practicing relaxation techniques can help introverts improve their sleep health and overall wellbeing.

Nutrition also plays a vital role in the physical health of introverts. A balanced diet that includes a variety of nutrients is essential for maintaining energy levels, supporting cognitive function, and promoting emotional stability. Introverts may benefit from mindful eating practices, which involve paying attention to hunger and fullness cues, choosing nutrient-dense foods, and avoiding emotional eating triggered by stress or social discomfort. Additionally, introverts can benefit from planning and preparing meals in a way that aligns with their preference for structure and predictability.

Social support is a crucial factor in the health and wellbeing of introverts. While introverts may prefer smaller social circles and deeper connections, having a network of supportive friends, family members, and colleagues is essential for their mental and emotional health. These relationships provide a sense of belonging, reduce feelings of isolation, and offer opportunities for meaningful interactions. Introverts can cultivate social support by investing in relationships that are mutually fulfilling, setting boundaries to ensure interactions are energizing rather than draining, and seeking out communities or groups that share their interests and values.

Work-life balance is another important consideration for introverts. Given their tendency to be thorough and detail-oriented, introverts may excel in roles that require focused, independent work. However, the demands of the modern workplace, including constant connectivity and collaborative tasks, can be challenging for introverts. To maintain their health and productivity, introverts need to create a work environment that accommodates their need for quiet and concentration. This can involve setting aside specific times for deep work, minimizing interruptions, and advocating for flexible work arrangements that allow for remote work or flexible hours.

Mindfulness and stress management practices are particularly beneficial for introverts, helping them navigate the challenges of overstimulation and social demands. Mindfulness techniques, such as meditation, deep breathing, and progressive muscle relaxation, can reduce stress, improve emotional regulation, and enhance overall wellbeing. Introverts can incorporate these practices into their daily routine to build resilience and maintain a sense of calm amidst the demands of daily life.

Creative outlets also play a significant role in the health of introverts. Engaging in creative activities such as writing, painting, music, or crafting provides an opportunity for self-expression and emotional processing. These activities can be deeply therapeutic, allowing introverts to channel their thoughts and feelings into productive and satisfying endeavors. Creating a dedicated space and time for creative pursuits can support introverts' mental and emotional health, providing a balance to the more structured and demanding aspects of their lives.

Nature and outdoor activities can offer restorative benefits for introverts. Spending time in natural settings, such as parks, forests, or near bodies of water, can reduce stress, improve mood, and enhance overall wellbeing. Introverts can benefit from incorporating regular outdoor activities into their routine, whether it's a daily walk in the park, gardening, or weekend hikes. The calming effects of nature can provide a counterbalance to the stimulation of urban environments and digital life.

Lastly, self-awareness and self-compassion are essential components of health for introverts. Understanding their own needs, strengths, and limitations allows introverts to make choices that support their wellbeing. This involves recognizing when they need solitude, setting boundaries to protect their energy, and seeking help when needed. Self-compassion involves treating themselves with kindness and understanding, particularly during times of stress or difficulty. By cultivating self-awareness and self-compassion, introverts can navigate the complexities of their personality and maintain their mental and physical health.

Chapter 27: Introverts in a Loud World

In a world that often celebrates extroversion and equates sociability with success, introverts can sometimes feel marginalized or pressured to conform to more outgoing norms. The journey of finding one's voice as an introvert in such a loud world involves understanding and embracing one's natural tendencies, leveraging unique strengths, and developing strategies to communicate effectively without sacrificing authenticity.

The societal preference for extroversion is evident in many aspects of life, from education and workplace environments to social expectations and media representations. Extroverted behaviors such as being outspoken, engaging in small talk, and thriving in group settings are often seen as desirable and indicative of confidence and leadership potential. This cultural bias can make introverts feel undervalued or pressured to emulate extroverted behaviors, which can be exhausting and counterproductive.

Understanding and embracing introversion is the first step for introverts to find their voice. Introversion is not a flaw or a limitation but a natural personality trait characterized by a preference for solitary activities, deep thinking, and meaningful interactions. Recognizing that introversion comes with its own set of strengths—such as the ability to focus deeply, think critically, and listen attentively—can help introverts appreciate their unique contributions. Embracing introversion involves rejecting the notion that they need to change to fit societal expectations and instead celebrating their authentic selves.

Self-acceptance is crucial for introverts to navigate a loud world. This involves acknowledging their preferences and needs without judgment and understanding that it is okay to seek solitude and recharge after social interactions. Introverts can practice self-compassion by recognizing that everyone has different ways of engaging with the world and that their approach is just as valid and valuable as any other. Self-acceptance also means setting boundaries and communicating their needs to others, whether it is requesting quiet time at home or advocating for a workspace that minimizes distractions.

One of the significant challenges for introverts is finding ways to communicate effectively in environments that favor extroverted communication styles. Public speaking, networking, and participating in group discussions can be daunting for introverts, who may prefer more reflective and one-on-one interactions. However, introverts can develop strategies to communicate confidently and effectively without compromising their natural inclinations.

Public speaking is often a major hurdle for introverts, but it is also a skill that can be mastered with practice and preparation. Introverts can excel in public speaking by leveraging their strengths in preparation and depth of knowledge. Preparing thoroughly, rehearsing the presentation multiple times, and structuring the content clearly can boost confidence and ensure a compelling delivery. Introverts can also use their natural ability to connect deeply with their audience by focusing on the message and the impact they want to create rather than on their own nervousness.

Networking is another area where introverts may feel out of their comfort zone, but they can approach it in ways that align with their preferences. Instead of trying to work the room at large events, introverts can seek out smaller gatherings or one-on-one meetings where they can engage in more meaningful conversations. They can also prepare questions and topics in advance to help guide the conversation and reduce anxiety. Building a network of trusted connections over time, rather than trying to accumulate a large number of acquaintances quickly, can be a more sustainable and satisfying approach for introverts.

In group discussions and meetings, introverts can find their voice by leveraging their listening skills and contributing thoughtfully. While they may not be the first to speak up, introverts can provide valuable insights by synthesizing the discussion and offering well-considered perspectives. Taking notes during the meeting can help introverts organize their thoughts and articulate their points more clearly. If speaking up in real-time is challenging, introverts can also follow up with written contributions or one-on-one discussions with key participants after the meeting.

Social media and digital communication offer introverts additional avenues to express themselves and connect with others. Platforms like blogs, forums, and social networks allow introverts to share their ideas and engage in discussions at their own pace and comfort level. Writing can be a powerful tool for introverts to articulate their thoughts and reach a wider audience without the immediate pressure of face-to-face interaction. By curating their online presence and participating in communities that align with their interests, introverts can find supportive networks and amplify their voice in ways that feel authentic and empowering.

Introverts can also find their voice by embracing and leveraging their natural strengths. Deep thinking and reflection enable introverts to generate original ideas and offer unique perspectives. By focusing on their areas of expertise and passion, introverts can build confidence and credibility in their chosen fields. Whether through writing, research, or creative projects, introverts can make significant contributions that resonate with others and establish their voice.

Collaboration is another area where introverts can shine by playing to their strengths. While they may prefer working independently, introverts can collaborate effectively by taking on roles that align with their skills, such as research, analysis, and project management. By working with others who complement their strengths, introverts can contribute to team success without feeling overwhelmed by constant social interaction. Clear communication and setting boundaries can help introverts manage collaborative efforts in a way that respects their need for solitude and focus.

Building resilience and coping strategies is essential for introverts to thrive in a loud world. This involves developing techniques to manage stress and recharge after social interactions. Practices such as mindfulness, meditation, and deep breathing can help introverts stay grounded and calm in high-stimulation environments. Regularly scheduling downtime and engaging in activities that bring joy and relaxation, such as reading, nature walks, or creative hobbies, can help introverts maintain their energy and well-being.

Mentorship and support networks can also play a crucial role in helping introverts find their voice. Connecting with other introverts or understanding mentors who appreciate their strengths can provide valuable guidance and encouragement. These relationships can offer a safe space to discuss challenges, share experiences, and receive constructive feedback. Support networks can also help introverts navigate professional and social environments by providing strategies and resources tailored to their needs.

Ultimately, finding one's voice as an introvert in a loud world involves a balance between self-acceptance and strategic action. Introverts can embrace their natural tendencies while also developing skills and strategies that enable them to communicate effectively and assertively. By recognizing their unique contributions, setting boundaries, leveraging their strengths, and seeking supportive relationships, introverts can navigate the demands of a loud world while staying true to themselves.

Chapter 28: The Role of Culture in Shaping Introversion

The role of culture in shaping introversion is a complex and multifaceted topic that examines how societal norms, values, and expectations influence the expression and perception of introverted traits. Introversion, as a personality characteristic, is universal, but the ways in which it is understood, valued, and manifested can vary significantly across different cultural contexts.

Culture encompasses the shared beliefs, customs, practices, and social behaviors of a particular group or society. It plays a crucial role in shaping how individuals perceive themselves and others, including personality traits such as introversion and extroversion. In many Western cultures, particularly in the United States, there is a strong cultural bias towards extroversion. Traits such as sociability, assertiveness, and gregariousness are often celebrated and seen as markers of success and leadership potential. This extroverted ideal is reinforced through various social institutions, including the educational system, workplace environments, and media representations.

In educational settings, for example, Western cultures often emphasize group work, class participation, and public speaking. Students who are naturally outgoing and comfortable in these settings are likely to be rewarded and recognized, while introverted students may struggle to meet these expectations. This can lead to a perception that introversion is a disadvantage or a deficiency that needs to be overcome. Introverted students may feel pressured to adopt more extroverted behaviors to succeed academically and socially, which can be stressful and exhausting.

Workplace environments in Western cultures also tend to favor extroverted traits. Open-plan offices, collaborative projects, and networking events are common features of many professional settings. Employees who are assertive, outgoing, and able to engage in small talk are often perceived as more competent and leadership-oriented. Introverted employees, on the other hand, may find these environments challenging and may be overlooked for promotions or leadership roles despite their skills and contributions. This can lead to a sense of frustration and undervaluation for introverted individuals.

Media representations further reinforce the extroverted ideal by frequently portraying successful individuals as charismatic, sociable, and outgoing. Television shows, movies, and advertisements often depict extroverted characters as heroes and role models, while introverted characters may be portrayed as shy, awkward, or antisocial. These portrayals can shape societal perceptions and self-perceptions, making it difficult for introverted individuals to see their traits as strengths.

In contrast to Western cultures, many Eastern cultures, particularly in Asia, have traditionally placed a higher value on introverted traits such as humility, modesty, and quiet reflection. In countries like Japan, China, and Korea, cultural norms often emphasize the importance of harmony, group cohesion, and respect for authority. In these contexts, introverted behaviors such as listening attentively, speaking modestly, and thinking deeply are often seen as signs of wisdom and respect. Introverted individuals may find it easier to navigate social and professional environments in these cultures, as their natural tendencies are more aligned with cultural expectations.

For example, in Japanese culture, the concept of "wa" (harmony) is highly valued, and individuals are encouraged to prioritize group harmony over individual expression. This cultural value can create a more supportive environment for introverted individuals, who may naturally excel in settings that require thoughtful listening and consensus-building. Similarly, in Chinese culture, the value of "ren" (benevolence) emphasizes the importance of humility and self-restraint, traits that are often associated with introversion. In these cultural contexts, introverted individuals may feel more accepted and valued for their contributions.

However, it is important to note that cultural attitudes towards introversion and extroversion are not static and can change over time. Globalization, technological advancements, and shifts in societal values can influence how introverted traits are perceived and valued in different cultures. For instance, as Western cultural influences spread through globalization, Eastern cultures may increasingly adopt more extroverted norms, particularly in urban and professional settings. Conversely, Western cultures may also begin to recognize and appreciate the value of introverted traits, especially as the understanding of diverse personality types grows.

The impact of cultural values on introverted individuals can be profound, affecting their self-esteem, mental health, and overall well-being. In cultures that prioritize extroversion, introverted individuals may feel marginalized or pressured to conform to extroverted norms. This pressure can lead to feelings of inadequacy, anxiety, and burnout. Introverted individuals may struggle to find environments where they can thrive and be themselves, leading to a sense of isolation and frustration.

On the other hand, in cultures that value introverted traits, introverted individuals may experience a greater sense of acceptance and validation. They may find it easier to navigate social and professional environments and may be more likely to receive recognition for their contributions. This cultural alignment can enhance their self-esteem and overall well-being, as they feel valued and respected for their natural tendencies.

Understanding the role of culture in shaping introversion is crucial for creating more inclusive and supportive environments. By recognizing and appreciating the diversity of personality traits, societies can foster a more inclusive culture that values both introverted and extroverted contributions. This involves challenging stereotypes and biases, promoting diverse representations in media, and creating spaces that accommodate different communication and interaction styles.

Educational institutions can play a significant role in this process by adopting teaching methods that cater to diverse learning styles and personality traits. For example, incorporating a mix of group work and independent projects, offering alternative forms of participation, and creating quiet spaces for reflection can help introverted students thrive. Educators can also encourage a culture of respect and appreciation for diverse contributions, highlighting the strengths and unique perspectives that introverted students bring to the classroom.

Workplace environments can also become more inclusive by recognizing the value of introverted traits and creating conditions that support diverse working styles. This can involve designing office spaces that offer both collaborative and quiet areas, implementing flexible work arrangements, and promoting a culture of respect for different communication styles. Leaders and managers can benefit from training on how to support and leverage the strengths of introverted employees, ensuring that they feel valued and have opportunities for growth and development.

Media representations can contribute to this cultural shift by showcasing diverse role models and challenging stereotypes. By depicting introverted characters as successful, confident, and influential, media can help reshape societal perceptions and validate the experiences of introverted individuals. This representation can empower introverted individuals to embrace their traits and recognize their potential for success and leadership.

On an individual level, introverted individuals can benefit from understanding how cultural influences shape their experiences and perceptions. This awareness can help them navigate social and professional environments more effectively, advocate for their needs, and find ways to express themselves authentically. Building a supportive network of like-minded individuals, seeking out environments that align with their values, and developing self-care practices can also enhance their well-being and resilience.

Chapter 29: The Quiet Writer

The role of the quiet writer in the literary world is a testament to the power of introspection, solitude, and deep reflection. Quiet writers, often introverts by nature, channel their thoughts and emotions into the written word, creating works that resonate with readers on a profound level.

Quiet writers typically find solace and inspiration in solitude. Unlike extroverted writers who may thrive on external stimuli and social interactions, quiet writers often seek the tranquility of their own company to delve deeply into their thoughts and ideas. This solitude allows them to explore their inner worlds, draw upon their rich inner lives, and create narratives that are nuanced, introspective, and deeply personal. In this space of quiet reflection, they can give voice to their innermost thoughts and emotions, crafting stories that speak to the universal human experience.

The writing process for quiet writers is often marked by meticulous attention to detail and a thoughtful, deliberate approach to storytelling. They may spend considerable time in contemplation, allowing ideas to gestate and mature before committing them to paper. This process of internal incubation is crucial for quiet writers, as it enables them to develop complex characters, intricate plots, and layered themes that resonate with authenticity and depth. Their narratives are often imbued with a sense of introspection and subtlety, inviting readers to engage in a reflective and contemplative reading experience.

One of the unique strengths of quiet writers is their ability to listen—both to themselves and to the world around them. This deep listening enables them to capture the nuances of human emotion and experience with precision and sensitivity. Whether they are writing fiction, poetry, essays, or memoirs, quiet writers excel at creating vivid, evocative descriptions that draw readers into the world of their characters. Their attention to detail and ability to observe the subtleties of life allow them to craft prose that is rich in imagery and emotional resonance.

Quiet writers often explore themes that reflect their introspective nature, such as identity, memory, solitude, and the passage of time. These themes are deeply personal and universal, allowing readers to see reflections of their own experiences and emotions in the writer's work. Through their exploration of these themes, quiet writers offer readers a mirror in which to examine their own lives, prompting reflection and self-discovery. Their writing serves as a conduit for exploring the complexities of the human condition, fostering empathy and understanding.

The challenges faced by quiet writers are manifold, particularly in a literary landscape that often values extroverted qualities such as self-promotion and public visibility. Quiet writers may struggle with the demands of marketing and networking, activities that require a level of extroversion that can be draining and uncomfortable for introverts. The pressure to engage in social media, attend literary events, and participate in public readings can be overwhelming for quiet writers, who may feel more at home in the solitude of their writing space.

Despite these challenges, quiet writers have found ways to navigate the demands of the literary world while staying true to their nature. Many have embraced the digital age, using blogs, websites, and social media platforms to share their work and connect with readers on their own terms. These platforms offer a way for quiet writers to reach a global audience without the need for constant face-to-face interaction. They can engage with readers through thoughtful posts, essays, and discussions, creating a community of like-minded individuals who appreciate their introspective approach to writing.

The impact of quiet writers on literature and society is profound and far-reaching. Their work often resonates deeply with readers who may feel marginalized or misunderstood, providing a sense of validation and connection. Quiet writers give voice to the experiences and emotions that are often overlooked or undervalued in a fast

-paced, extroverted world. By sharing their inner worlds, quiet writers create a space for introspection and reflection, encouraging readers to slow down and engage with their own thoughts and feelings.

The literary contributions of quiet writers are diverse and significant. They have produced some of the most enduring and beloved works of literature, offering insights into the human experience that transcend time and place. Authors such as Emily Dickinson, Franz Kafka, J.D. Salinger, Virginia Woolf, and Haruki Murakami, among many others, have captivated readers with their introspective and deeply personal narratives. These writers have used their quiet voices to explore themes of alienation, identity, and the search for meaning, creating works that resonate with readers across generations.

Emily Dickinson, for example, is often celebrated for her reclusive nature and the profound depth of her poetry. Living much of her life in relative seclusion, Dickinson's poetry reflects her keen observation of the world and her rich inner life. Her works, characterized by their brevity and intensity, delve into themes of death, immortality, and the natural world, offering readers a glimpse into her unique perspective.

Franz Kafka, another quintessential quiet writer, used his introspective nature to craft stories that explore the absurdity and alienation of modern life. Kafka's works, such as "The Metamorphosis" and "The Trial," are marked by their surreal and unsettling qualities, reflecting his inner anxieties and existential reflections. His ability to capture the human condition's complexity and strangeness has left a lasting impact on literature and continues to inspire readers and writers alike.

J.D. Salinger, known for his iconic novel "The Catcher in the Rye," captured the voice of a generation with his portrayal of teenage angst and alienation. Salinger's reclusive lifestyle and reluctance to engage with the public only added to the mystique of his work, highlighting the tension between personal privacy and public attention that many quiet writers experience.

Virginia Woolf's stream-of-consciousness writing style and exploration of the inner lives of her characters have made her a seminal figure in modernist literature. In works like "Mrs. Dalloway" and "To the Lighthouse," Woolf delves into the complexities of human consciousness, memory, and time, offering readers a rich tapestry of thought and emotion. Her introspective approach has paved the way for future writers to explore the intricacies of the mind and the human experience.

Haruki Murakami, a contemporary quiet writer, blends elements of magical realism, surrealism, and introspection in his novels. Works such as "Norwegian Wood" and "Kafka on the Shore" delve into themes of loneliness, self-discovery, and the blurred lines between reality and fantasy. Murakami's unique voice and ability to tap into the subconscious have earned him a dedicated global readership.

The quiet writer's influence extends beyond individual works to shape broader literary movements and trends. The introspective nature of their writing often leads to innovations in narrative structure, character development, and thematic exploration. By prioritizing depth over breadth and reflection over action, quiet writers challenge readers to engage more deeply with the text and to consider the subtler aspects of the human experience.

The impact of quiet writers on readers is equally profound. Their work often provides solace and companionship to those who feel out of step with the extroverted norms of society. Readers who identify with the introspective nature of quiet writers find validation and understanding in their works, creating a sense of connection that transcends the written word. The themes explored by quiet writers—such as identity, solitude, and the search for meaning—resonate deeply with readers who are grappling with similar issues in their own lives.

Quiet writers also play a crucial role in fostering empathy and understanding. By offering a window into their inner worlds, they allow readers to see the world from different perspectives and to appreciate the diversity of human experience. This ability to evoke empathy is particularly important in an increasingly fragmented and polarized world, where understanding and connection are more vital than ever.

In addition to their literary contributions, quiet writers often serve as advocates for the value of introspection and solitude. In a culture that prizes constant activity and social engagement, quiet writers remind us of the importance of taking time to reflect, to think deeply, and to connect with our inner selves. Their work encourages readers to slow down, to listen to their own thoughts and emotions, and to find meaning in stillness and silence.

The challenges faced by quiet writers are significant, but their contributions to literature and society are invaluable. By embracing their introspective nature and finding ways to navigate the demands of the literary world, quiet writers continue to create works that resonate with readers and inspire future generations of writers. Their ability to express complex and nuanced thoughts through the written word is a testament to the power of introspection and the enduring value of the quiet voice in a loud world.

Chapter 30: The Introvert's Social Calendar

The social calendar of an introvert is a finely tuned instrument that balances the need for solitude with the desire for meaningful social interaction. For introverts, planning social activities requires thoughtful consideration to ensure that their need for downtime is respected while also fostering connections with others.

At the heart of an introvert's approach to social planning is the understanding that social interactions, while valuable, can be draining. Unlike extroverts, who often gain energy from being around others, introverts typically expend energy in social settings. As a result, they need to carefully manage their time and energy to avoid burnout and maintain their well-being. This requires a deep awareness of their own limits and a proactive approach to scheduling social activities.

One of the key strategies introverts use to plan their social calendars is prioritizing quality over quantity. Rather than filling their schedules with numerous social engagements, introverts tend to be selective about the activities they commit to. They often prefer smaller, more intimate gatherings where meaningful conversations and connections can take place. These settings allow introverts to engage more deeply with others without the overwhelming stimulation of large groups.

To maintain a balanced social calendar, introverts often plan their activities well in advance. This allows them to ensure that they have sufficient downtime between social engagements. For example, an introvert might schedule a quiet evening at home or a solitary walk in nature after attending a social event. This intentional planning helps them recharge and prepare for the next social interaction. By spacing out their social activities, introverts can avoid the fatigue and stress that can come from back-to-back engagements.

Introverts also benefit from setting boundaries and managing expectations with friends and family. Communicating their need for downtime and alone time can help others understand their behavior and reduce any potential misunderstandings. For instance, an introvert might explain to their friends that they need to leave a party early or that they prefer smaller gatherings over large celebrations. Setting these boundaries helps introverts maintain their energy levels and enjoy social interactions on their own terms.

The types of social activities introverts prefer often reflect their need for meaningful and low-stimulation environments. Quiet dinners with close friends, book clubs, nature hikes, and one-on-one coffee dates are examples of activities that introverts might find enjoyable and fulfilling. These settings allow for deeper connections and conversations without the sensory overload that can come from crowded or noisy environments.

Another aspect of planning a comfortable social calendar involves finding activities that align with an introvert's interests and passions. Engaging in activities that they genuinely enjoy can make social interactions more enjoyable and less draining. For example, an introvert who loves art might enjoy visiting a museum with a friend, or an introvert who enjoys writing might participate in a writing workshop. By focusing on activities that bring them joy and fulfillment, introverts can create positive social experiences that energize rather than deplete them.

Introverts may also benefit from creating social rituals and routines that provide structure and predictability. For example, having a regular monthly dinner with a close friend or a weekly phone call with a family member can provide a sense of stability and comfort. These rituals can help introverts maintain their social connections without feeling overwhelmed by the need to constantly plan and organize new activities.

While introverts often prefer smaller, quieter settings, it is important to recognize that they can still enjoy larger social events, provided they are approached with care. For example, an introvert attending a large party or networking event might plan to stay for a limited amount of time, allowing themselves the option to leave early if they start to feel drained. They might also identify quieter areas where they can retreat for a break or spend time with a smaller group of people within the larger event.

The challenges faced by introverts in managing their social calendars are multifaceted. One common challenge is balancing the desire for social connection with the need for solitude. Introverts may feel torn between wanting to spend time with friends and family and needing time alone to recharge. This internal conflict can lead to feelings of guilt or social anxiety, particularly if they feel pressured to conform to extroverted social norms.

Another challenge is navigating social expectations and obligations. Introverts may feel obligated to attend social events out of a sense of duty or to avoid disappointing others. This can lead to overcommitment and burnout if they do not set clear boundaries and prioritize their own needs. Learning to say no gracefully and assertively is a crucial skill for introverts to develop, allowing them to protect their energy and well-being.

Social anxiety is another significant challenge that many introverts face. The prospect of social interactions can be daunting, leading to feelings of nervousness, self-doubt, and fear of judgment. To cope with social anxiety, introverts can use various strategies, such as preparing for social interactions in advance, practicing relaxation techniques, and gradually exposing themselves to social situations to build confidence. Seeking support from a therapist or counselor can also be beneficial for managing social anxiety and developing coping strategies.

Despite these challenges, introverts can create a fulfilling and comfortable social life by embracing their unique strengths and preferences. One of the key strengths of introverts is their ability to form deep and meaningful connections with others. By focusing on quality relationships rather than quantity, introverts can cultivate a supportive and nurturing social network. These close relationships provide a sense of belonging and connection that is vital for emotional well-being.

Another strength of introverts is their ability to listen and empathize. Introverts often excel at active listening, providing their friends and loved ones with a sense of being truly heard and understood. This ability to listen deeply and empathetically can strengthen relationships and create a sense of intimacy and trust. By leveraging this strength, introverts can build strong and lasting connections with others.

Introverts can also benefit from embracing their need for solitude and self-care. Recognizing that alone time is essential for their well-being, introverts can prioritize self-care practices that help them recharge and maintain their energy levels. This might include activities such as reading, journaling, meditation, or spending time in nature. By honoring their need for solitude, introverts can ensure that they are able to show up fully and authentically in their social interactions.

Technology can also play a role in helping introverts manage their social calendars. Social media, messaging apps, and online communities provide introverts with alternative ways to connect with others without the need for constant face-to-face interaction. Virtual book clubs, online support groups, and social networks can offer introverts a sense of community and connection while allowing them to engage on their own terms. However, it is important for introverts to set boundaries with technology to avoid overstimulation and digital fatigue.

In addition to technology, introverts can explore creative ways to connect with others that align with their preferences. For example, hosting small, themed gatherings or organizing activities that have a clear purpose and structure can make social interactions more enjoyable and less stressful. Participating in volunteer work or joining interest-based groups can also provide opportunities for meaningful social engagement in a comfortable and supportive environment.

Lastly, introverts can benefit from cultivating self-compassion and self-acceptance. Recognizing that their need for solitude and introspection is a natural and valuable aspect of their personality can help introverts feel more confident and at ease in their social interactions. By embracing their introversion and understanding that it is not a flaw but a unique strength, introverts can approach their social calendars with a sense of empowerment and authenticity.

Chapter 31: The Quiet Traveler

Traveling, often seen as a quintessentially social and extroverted activity, holds unique and profound possibilities for introverts. The quiet traveler embarks on journeys that are not just about the destinations but also about the introspective experiences, personal growth, and deep connections with the world around them. For introverts, exploring the world their way means creating travel experiences that align with their need for solitude, contemplation, and meaningful engagement.

At the core of the quiet traveler's approach is the preference for solo travel or small group adventures. Traveling alone allows introverts to set their own pace, make spontaneous decisions, and spend time in reflection without the pressure of social obligations. Solo travel provides the freedom to immerse oneself fully in the experience, whether that means spending hours in a museum, wandering through quiet streets, or sitting by the ocean lost in thought. For introverts, this autonomy is invaluable, as it enables them to recharge and enjoy their travels in a way that is most fulfilling to them.

When traveling with others, introverts often prefer the company of a small, close-knit group of friends or family members. Such groups offer a balance of companionship and personal space, allowing introverts to enjoy shared experiences without feeling overwhelmed by constant social interaction. Traveling with a small group also makes it easier to find consensus on activities and schedules that accommodate everyone's preferences, including the introvert's need for downtime.

Introverts often seek out destinations that offer tranquility and opportunities for deep engagement with the environment. Natural settings such as mountains, forests, beaches, and rural landscapes are particularly appealing. These places provide a sense of peace and solitude, allowing introverts to connect with nature and recharge away from the hustle and bustle of urban life. The beauty and serenity of nature can be a profound source of inspiration and introspection, making it an ideal backdrop for the quiet traveler.

Cultural and historical destinations also hold great appeal for introverts. Places rich in history and cultural heritage offer numerous opportunities for quiet exploration and learning. Museums, historical sites, art galleries, and libraries are havens where introverts can delve into the stories and artifacts of the past. These environments often provide a calm and contemplative atmosphere, perfect for introspective travelers. Additionally, experiencing different cultures and ways of life can broaden an introvert's perspective and deepen their understanding of the world.

For introverts, planning is a key aspect of a successful travel experience. Detailed research and preparation allow them to anticipate and mitigate potential stressors. This might include booking accommodations that offer privacy and quiet, such as boutique hotels, bed and breakfasts, or vacation rentals. These options provide a more personal and peaceful environment compared to large, crowded hotels. Introverts may also look for accommodations that have common areas where they can relax without the pressure of socializing, such as gardens, lounges, or libraries.

Careful planning extends to the itinerary as well. Introverts often prefer a slower travel pace, with fewer activities each day to allow for ample downtime and spontaneous exploration. Creating an itinerary that includes a mix of structured activities and free time ensures that introverts can enjoy the highlights of their destination without feeling rushed or exhausted. They may also prioritize activities that align with their interests and passions, such as attending a classical music concert, taking a cooking class, or exploring local markets and bookstores.

Despite their preference for solitude, introverts can also find joy in connecting with others during their travels, particularly through meaningful interactions rather than casual small talk. Engaging with locals, learning about their customs and way of life, and sharing stories can be deeply enriching experiences. Introverts may find it easier to connect with others in settings that promote genuine conversation, such as homestays, guided tours with small groups, or volunteering opportunities. These interactions can provide a sense of connection and community without the overwhelm of constant socializing.

Technology can be a valuable tool for the quiet traveler. Apps and websites that offer travel guides, language translation, and navigation can help introverts feel more confident and self-sufficient while exploring new places. Social media and travel blogs provide inspiration and practical tips from like-minded travelers, while online communities can offer support and advice. However, introverts should also be mindful of their digital consumption, ensuring that they remain present and fully engaged in their travel experiences.

One of the greatest benefits of travel for introverts is the opportunity for personal growth and self-discovery. Traveling pushes introverts out of their comfort zones, challenging them to navigate unfamiliar environments, adapt to new situations, and interact with diverse groups of people. These experiences can build confidence, resilience, and a sense of independence. The introspective nature of introverts allows them to reflect deeply on their experiences, leading to greater self-awareness and personal insight.

Traveling can also be a form of healing and rejuvenation for introverts. The change of scenery, the break from routine, and the immersion in new environments can provide a much-needed reset. Whether it's finding solace in nature, drawing inspiration from art and history, or simply enjoying the peace and quiet of a secluded beach, travel can restore an introvert's energy and well-being. It offers a chance to disconnect from the demands of daily life and reconnect with oneself.

While the quiet traveler seeks peace and introspection, they also recognize the value of balance. Too much solitude can lead to feelings of isolation, so it's important for introverts to find ways to engage with others and create meaningful social connections. This might include joining group activities that align with their interests, such as a photography workshop, a hiking tour, or a cultural festival. These shared experiences can foster a sense of camaraderie and provide opportunities for authentic interaction.

The quiet traveler's journey is also about embracing the unexpected and finding joy in the small moments. Introverts often have a heightened awareness of their surroundings, allowing them to notice the subtle beauty and details that others might overlook. Whether it's savoring a quiet moment in a charming café, watching the sunrise over a tranquil landscape, or simply wandering through a quiet village, these experiences can be deeply enriching and memorable.

Chapter 32: The Future of Introversion

The future of introversion is an intriguing and multifaceted topic that encompasses societal trends, technological advancements, workplace dynamics, educational shifts, and cultural changes. As society evolves, the understanding and appreciation of introversion are likely to deepen, leading to a more inclusive environment that recognizes the unique strengths and needs of introverts.

One of the most significant trends impacting the future of introversion is the increasing recognition and validation of different personality types. In recent years, there has been a growing awareness of the diversity of human temperaments, largely influenced by the popularization of personality psychology, such as the Myers-Briggs Type Indicator (MBTI) and the work of psychologists like Carl Jung and Susan Cain. Cain's book "Quiet: The Power of Introverts in a World That Can't Stop Talking" has played a pivotal role in bringing introversion into the mainstream consciousness. This shift towards understanding and appreciating introversion is likely to continue, fostering a more inclusive society that values the contributions of introverts.

Technological advancements will play a crucial role in shaping the future of introversion. The rise of remote work, accelerated by the COVID-19 pandemic, has highlighted the advantages of flexible work environments. Remote work provides introverts with the opportunity to work in settings that are less stimulating and more conducive to their productivity. As companies recognize the benefits of remote and hybrid work models, it is likely that these options will become more widely available, allowing introverts to thrive in their professional roles without the constant pressure of in-person interactions.

Moreover, advancements in communication technology are expected to further support introverts. Tools such as video conferencing, instant messaging, and collaborative platforms enable introverts to engage with colleagues and participate in meetings without the stress of face-to-face interactions. These technologies also allow for asynchronous communication, giving introverts the time they need to process information and respond thoughtfully. As virtual and augmented reality technologies continue to develop, they may offer new ways for introverts to engage in social and professional interactions in a more controlled and comfortable environment.

The future workplace is likely to become more introvert-friendly as organizations recognize the importance of accommodating different working styles. Companies are increasingly focusing on creating diverse and inclusive work environments, which includes understanding and supporting introverted employees. This may involve designing office spaces with quiet areas, offering flexible work arrangements, and promoting a culture that values deep work and thoughtful contributions. Leadership training programs may also begin to emphasize the strengths of introverted leaders, such as their ability to listen, think critically, and make well-considered decisions.

In the realm of education, there is a growing movement towards personalized learning, which can greatly benefit introverted students. Traditional educational models that emphasize group work and constant interaction can be challenging for introverts. However, with the rise of online learning platforms and adaptive learning technologies, education can be tailored to meet the needs of individual students. Personalized learning allows introverts to engage with material at their own pace and in their preferred style, whether that means spending more time on independent study or participating in smaller, focused discussion groups. This approach can help introverted students thrive academically and develop confidence in their abilities.

Cultural shifts are also expected to play a role in shaping the future of introversion. As global connectivity increases, there is greater exposure to different cultures and ways of life. Some cultures, particularly in Eastern societies, traditionally place a higher value on traits associated with introversion, such as humility, restraint, and contemplation. As these cultural values become more recognized and appreciated globally, there may be a broader acceptance of introverted traits. This cultural exchange can lead to a more balanced understanding of personality types and reduce the stigma associated with introversion in traditionally extroverted societies.

Social media and digital communities will continue to provide introverts with platforms to express themselves and connect with others on their own terms. While social media can be overwhelming, it also offers introverts the ability to engage in meaningful conversations, share their thoughts, and build relationships without the immediate pressures of face-to-face interaction. Niche online communities, such as forums and interest-based groups, allow introverts to connect with like-minded individuals and find support. As these digital spaces evolve, they may offer even more opportunities for introverts to engage in enriching and fulfilling social interactions.

The future of introversion also holds potential for greater recognition of the mental health needs of introverts. The connection between introversion and mental health is complex, with introverts sometimes experiencing higher levels of social anxiety and overstimulation. As mental health awareness continues to grow, there will likely be more resources and support available to help introverts manage these challenges. This could include access to therapy, mindfulness and relaxation techniques, and tools for managing sensory input. Employers and educators may also become more attuned to the mental health needs of introverts, creating environments that reduce stress and promote well-being.

In the field of entertainment and media, there is a trend towards more nuanced and diverse representations of personality types. As storytellers and content creators strive to reflect the real world more accurately, introverted characters are being portrayed in more complex and positive ways. This shift can help to change societal perceptions of introversion, showcasing the strengths and inner lives of introverted individuals. In the future, we can expect to see more films, books, and TV shows that highlight the unique perspectives and contributions of introverts, further validating and normalizing introversion.

Advancements in artificial intelligence (AI) and data analytics may also offer new insights into introversion. AI-powered tools can analyze large datasets to identify patterns and trends in behavior, preferences, and communication styles. This information can be used to develop personalized solutions that cater to the needs of introverts, whether in education, healthcare, or the workplace. For example, AI could help create customized learning plans for students or develop workplace policies that support different working styles. These technologies have the potential to enhance the understanding and accommodation of introversion on a broader scale.

As society becomes more attuned to environmental sustainability, the emphasis on slow living and minimalism may resonate with introverted values. The slow living movement, which encourages a more mindful and deliberate approach to life, aligns with the introvert's preference for depth over breadth. Minimalism, with its focus on reducing unnecessary stimulation and clutter, can create environments that are more conducive to the introvert's need for calm and order. These lifestyle trends can support introverts in creating spaces and routines that enhance their well-being and allow them to thrive.

In terms of personal development, the future may see a greater emphasis on self-awareness and emotional intelligence. As people become more interested in understanding their own personalities and those of others, tools and resources for personal growth will continue to evolve. Workshops, retreats, and courses focused on self-discovery and interpersonal skills can help introverts better understand their strengths and how to navigate a predominantly extroverted world. This increased self-awareness can empower introverts to advocate for their needs and make choices that align with their true selves.

The future of introversion also holds promise for greater societal acceptance of diverse communication styles. The increasing recognition of neurodiversity highlights the importance of accommodating different ways of thinking and interacting. Introverts, who may prefer written communication or one-on-one conversations, can benefit from environments that respect and value these preferences. As workplaces and educational institutions become more inclusive, there will likely be a broader acceptance of various communication styles, reducing the pressure on introverts to conform to extroverted norms.

Chapter 33: Balancing Act

The concept of balancing introversion and extroversion within oneself is a profound and nuanced subject, touching on the complexities of human personality and the ways in which individuals navigate their social and inner worlds. This balancing act involves recognizing and integrating both introverted and extroverted traits, understanding their interplay, and leveraging them to achieve personal harmony and effective functioning in various aspects of life.

At the core of this balancing act is the recognition that introversion and extroversion exist on a spectrum rather than as binary opposites. Carl Jung, the Swiss psychiatrist who first popularized the terms, described introversion and extroversion as two poles of a continuum, with individuals often exhibiting a mix of both traits. While some people may lean more heavily towards one end of the spectrum, most people possess a combination of introverted and extroverted tendencies. Understanding this spectrum is crucial for appreciating the dynamic nature of personality and the potential for individuals to adapt and thrive in different contexts.

Introversion is characterized by a preference for solitary activities, a focus on internal thoughts and feelings, and a tendency to find social interactions draining. Introverts often enjoy deep, meaningful conversations, introspection, and activities that allow for contemplation and creativity. They may feel overwhelmed by large crowds or excessive stimulation and typically require time alone to recharge their energy.

Extroversion, on the other hand, is associated with a preference for social interaction, external focus, and a tendency to gain energy from being around others. Extroverts thrive in social settings, enjoy meeting new people, and are often more outspoken and assertive. They may feel energized by group activities and external stimuli and often seek out opportunities for social engagement and excitement.

For many individuals, balancing these traits involves recognizing the situations in which each tendency serves them best and developing strategies to integrate both aspects of their personality. This process of self-awareness and adaptation can lead to a more fulfilling and balanced life, as individuals learn to harness their strengths and address their challenges.

One effective strategy for balancing introversion and extroversion is to identify and honor one's natural preferences while also challenging oneself to step out of the comfort zone. For example, an individual who identifies primarily as an introvert might recognize the value of social interactions for personal and professional growth and make a conscious effort to engage in networking events, social gatherings, or collaborative projects. Conversely, an extrovert might recognize the benefits of solitude for reflection, creativity, and stress reduction and make time for solitary activities such as reading, journaling, or meditation.

Creating a balanced lifestyle involves structuring one's environment and daily routine to accommodate both introverted and extroverted needs. This might include setting aside specific times for social activities and solitude, ensuring that both are given equal importance. For instance, an introvert who enjoys socializing might plan regular outings with friends but also schedule quiet evenings at home to recharge. An extrovert who thrives on social interaction might incorporate solitary activities into their routine, such as a morning walk or an afternoon of focused work, to maintain balance and avoid burnout.

Mindfulness and self-reflection are powerful tools for achieving this balance. Regularly assessing one's energy levels, emotional state, and social needs can help individuals make informed decisions about how to allocate their time and energy. This practice can involve keeping a journal to track social interactions and solitary activities, noting how each affects one's mood and energy levels, and making adjustments as needed.

Another important aspect of balancing introversion and extroversion is developing effective communication skills. Understanding and articulating one's needs to others can foster mutual respect and understanding in relationships. For example, an introvert might explain to a friend or partner that they need some alone time to recharge after a busy day, while an extrovert might express the importance of social activities for their well-being. Open and honest communication can help manage expectations and create a supportive environment for both introverted and extroverted tendencies.

In the workplace, balancing introversion and extroversion can enhance productivity, creativity, and collaboration. Introverts may excel in roles that require deep concentration, analytical thinking, and independent work, while extroverts may thrive in positions that involve teamwork, public speaking, and social interaction. Recognizing these strengths and creating opportunities for employees to work in ways that suit their preferences can lead to a more harmonious and effective work environment. Employers can support this balance by offering flexible work arrangements, such as remote work or flexible hours, providing quiet spaces for focused work, and fostering a culture that values diverse communication styles and contributions.

Balancing introversion and extroversion also have significant implications for personal relationships. In romantic relationships, partners with different personality traits can complement each other, bringing a balance of energy and perspective. However, this requires understanding and appreciating each other's needs and finding ways to meet them. For example, a couple might plan a mix of social outings and quiet evenings at home, ensuring that both partners feel satisfied and understood. In friendships, respecting each other's boundaries and preferences can strengthen the bond and create a more supportive and fulfilling relationship.

For parents and educators, recognizing and nurturing both introverted and extroverted traits in children is crucial for their development and well-being. Encouraging children to explore a variety of activities, both social and solitary, can help them discover their strengths and interests. Providing opportunities for children to engage in group activities, as well as offering quiet time for reflection and creativity, can foster a balanced and well-rounded personality. Understanding that children may have different needs and preferences can help create a supportive environment that allows them to thrive.

The process of balancing introversion and extroversion also involves acknowledging and addressing the challenges associated with each trait. Introverts may need to develop strategies for managing social anxiety, building confidence in social settings, and preventing isolation. This might involve practicing social skills, gradually exposing oneself to social situations, and seeking support from a therapist or counselor. Extroverts, on the other hand, may need to learn how to enjoy solitude, manage overstimulation, and develop patience and listening skills. Techniques such as mindfulness meditation, setting aside time for quiet reflection, and practicing active listening can help extroverts cultivate these abilities.

As society becomes more aware of the diversity of personality types, there is a growing recognition of the value of both introverted and extroverted traits. This shift towards greater acceptance and appreciation of different temperaments can create a more inclusive and supportive environment for everyone. Educational institutions, workplaces, and communities can play a vital role in fostering this acceptance by promoting awareness and understanding of introversion and extroversion and creating spaces that accommodate diverse needs and preferences.

Chapter 34: Celebrating the Quiet Spectrum

Celebrating the quiet spectrum involves embracing the full range of introverted qualities and recognizing the value that these traits bring to both individuals and society as a whole. This celebration is about acknowledging the strengths inherent in introversion, dismantling the societal biases that often favor extroverted characteristics, and cultivating an environment where introverts can thrive authentically. By exploring the nuances of introversion and encouraging self-acceptance, we can better appreciate the diverse ways people contribute to the world.

The concept of the quiet spectrum highlights the idea that introversion is not a monolithic trait but rather a continuum of behaviors and preferences. Some individuals may be deeply introverted, finding joy and energy in solitude and quiet reflection, while others may fall closer to the middle of the spectrum, enjoying both social interactions and alone time in balanced measures. Understanding that introversion exists on a spectrum allows for a more nuanced appreciation of the various ways introverts engage with the world.

One of the fundamental aspects of celebrating the quiet spectrum is recognizing the strengths and unique qualities that introverts bring to the table. Introverts are often deeply reflective, able to think critically and creatively about complex issues. Their capacity for deep focus and concentration allows them to delve into subjects with a level of thoroughness that can lead to innovative solutions and insights. In a world that often values quick, surface-level thinking, the depth of thought that introverts offer is invaluable.

Furthermore, introverts typically excel in one-on-one and small group interactions, where they can form meaningful, lasting connections. Their preference for deep, authentic conversations over superficial small talk enables them to build strong, trust-based relationships. In professional settings, this can translate into effective teamwork, mentorship, and leadership, as introverts often bring a calm, thoughtful presence to group dynamics. By fostering environments that encourage and respect these interactions, we can harness the full potential of introverts.

Empathy and active listening are also hallmarks of introversion. Introverts often have a heightened sensitivity to the emotions and experiences of others, which makes them excellent listeners and supportive friends. This empathy extends to their professional lives, where they can build inclusive, understanding workplaces. By creating spaces where introverts can leverage their empathetic skills, we not only benefit from their individual contributions but also foster a more compassionate, collaborative culture.

Despite these strengths, societal biases often favor extroverted qualities such as assertiveness, sociability, and high energy. This bias can make it challenging for introverts to feel valued and understood. Celebrating the quiet spectrum involves actively working to dismantle these biases and promoting a more inclusive understanding of success and contribution. This can be achieved through education, raising awareness about the value of introverted traits, and creating policies and practices that accommodate different working styles and preferences.

Self-acceptance is a critical component of embracing the quiet spectrum. Introverts often feel pressure to conform to extroverted norms, which can lead to feelings of inadequacy or inauthenticity. Encouraging introverts to embrace their true selves involves validating their experiences and preferences and helping them to see the value in their way of being. This might include practicing self-compassion, setting boundaries to protect their energy, and seeking out environments and activities that align with their natural inclinations.

Creating supportive environments for introverts involves both physical and social considerations. On a physical level, designing spaces that offer quiet, private areas where introverts can retreat and recharge is essential. This might include quiet rooms in workplaces, libraries, or community centers. On a social level, fostering a culture that respects different communication styles and interaction preferences is crucial. This can be achieved through practices such as allowing for written communication options, offering flexible work arrangements, and valuing deep, reflective contributions as much as those made in more spontaneous settings.

Another important aspect of celebrating the quiet spectrum is encouraging introverts to explore and develop their unique interests and passions. Introverts often thrive in environments where they can immerse themselves in subjects that fascinate them. Whether it's pursuing a creative hobby, engaging in scientific research, or becoming involved in community service, finding activities that resonate deeply can provide a sense of fulfillment and purpose. By supporting introverts in these pursuits, we can help them to shine in their own way.

Building a community of like-minded individuals can also be incredibly empowering for introverts. Connecting with other introverts who understand and appreciate their experiences can provide a sense of belonging and validation. This might involve joining or forming groups centered around shared interests, participating in online communities, or attending events designed specifically for introverts. These connections can offer support, inspiration, and opportunities for collaboration, further enhancing the sense of celebration and empowerment.

Education and advocacy play a significant role in celebrating the quiet spectrum on a broader scale. Educating others about the strengths and contributions of introverts helps to challenge stereotypes and promote a more inclusive understanding of personality. Advocacy efforts can include pushing for changes in workplace policies, educational practices, and social norms that better accommodate and celebrate introverted traits. By raising awareness and advocating for change, we can create a society that values and respects the full spectrum of human experiences.

Role models and public figures who identify as introverts can also inspire and empower others. When successful introverts share their stories and strategies for navigating the world, they provide valuable insights and encouragement. These role models demonstrate that it is possible to achieve great things while staying true to one's introverted nature. Celebrating their achievements helps to normalize and validate the experiences of introverts everywhere.

Epilogue

As we come to the end of our exploration into "The Quiet Spectrum: The Thought Patterns of Introverts," it is clear that introversion is not a limitation but a profound and diverse strength. Throughout these pages, we have journeyed through the intricate landscapes of the introverted mind, uncovering the hidden depths and quiet power that define so many.

Introversion is a celebration of inner life—a testament to the beauty of deep thought, careful reflection, and meaningful connection. It is a reminder that silence and solitude are not voids to be filled but spaces where creativity blooms and wisdom grows. By understanding and embracing the quiet spectrum, we unlock the potential to live authentically and harmoniously in a world that often feels overwhelmingly loud.

To the introverts reading this book: may you now see your quiet nature as a strength, not a shortcoming. May you embrace your need for solitude without guilt, knowing that it is in these moments that your best ideas and deepest insights take shape. Remember that your reflective nature allows you to see the world with clarity and empathy, qualities that are invaluable in every sphere of life.

To the extroverts: may you have gained a deeper appreciation for the introverted individuals in your life. Recognize the value of their perspective, their ability to listen, and their thoughtfulness. By bridging the gap between introversion and extroversion, we create a more inclusive and understanding world where every voice, loud or quiet, is heard and valued.

The journey of understanding introversion does not end with this book. It continues in everyday interactions, in the way we structure our lives, and in the respect, we afford each other's differences. By fostering environments where introverts can thrive—whether in schools, workplaces, or social settings—we contribute to a richer, more balanced society.

In this fast-paced world, it is vital to remember the importance of pause and reflection. The quiet spectrum teaches us that there is immense power in stillness, that true connection often happens in moments of silence, and that sometimes, the most profound changes begin within.

Thank you for embarking on this journey with me. May "The Quiet Spectrum" serve as a guide and a companion as you continue to navigate the complexities of introversion. Celebrate your quiet moments, cherish your deep thoughts, and know that in the spectrum of human experience, your voice—however softly spoken—makes a significant impact.

The End.

www.ingramcontent.com/pod-product-compliance
Lightning Source LLC
Chambersburg PA
CBHW062141150726

47991CB00006B/2139